"*In Their Shoes* is a must-have resource for any stepparent. While spending time with Lauren Reitsema, I have been very impacted by her wisdom and insight—and I know you will be, too. In this book, using real-life examples, Lauren uncovers the unspoken feelings of stepchildren and explains the 'why' behind them. For most stepparents, having your eyes opened to what you simply didn't see before will be the key to unlocking your relationship!"

—Shaunti Feldhahn, social researcher and bestselling author
of *For Women Only* and *The Kindness Challenge*

"*In Their Shoes* should be required reading for every parent, coach, and educator who cares for children of divorce. Our culture has seen a silent epidemic of countless children suffering with invisible wounds caused by living through the aftermath of divorce. Lauren Reitsema has pulled the curtain back and given us a peek into the lives of kids who are navigating the emotional complexities of growing up in post-divorce homes and in blended families. From her personal experiences, gripping true stories, and insightful research, Lauren has masterfully created a resource to equip families, heal deep wounds, and empower children navigating the aftermath of divorce for generations to come!"

—Dave and Ashley Willis, authors, relationship coaches,
and TV hosts for *MarriageToday*

IN THEIR SHOES

SMART
STEPFAMILY
SERIES

Books in the SMART STEPFAMILY Series

IN THEIR SHOES

Helping Parents Better Understand
and Connect with Children of Divorce

LAUREN REITSEMA

BETHANYHOUSE
a division of Baker Publishing Group
Minneapolis, Minnesota

Published by Bethany House Publishers
11400 Hampshire Avenue South
Bloomington, Minnesota 55438
www.bethanyhouse.com

Bethany House Publishers is a division of
Baker Publishing Group, Grand Rapids, Michigan

Printed in the United States of America

ISBN 978-0-7642-3301-2
Library of Congress Control Number: 2019021045

Cover design by Kara Klontz

19 20 21 22 23 24 25   7 6 5 4 3 2 1

For every child who has
packed a suitcase to go home.

For Josh, Lia, Jace, and Nina Jo
I'm home wherever you are.

Contents

Foreword

I have advocated for the publication of this book since Lauren and I first met. Let me tell you why.

While headed to a speaking engagement, I began talking with a young woman sitting beside me on the airplane. Or perhaps I should say, she started talking to me. After glancing at my laptop and noticing that I was preparing a presentation on blended families, she started asking questions.

What's your presentation about?

Who is your conference for?

How did you get into this?

Once she learned that I was an author and family therapist who specialized in working with stepfamilies, she asked one more question that took me aback.

What kind of psychological issues come with being from a stepfamily?

I've learned that most direct questions, like this one, arise out of someone's life experience. I wasn't sure exactly where she was coming from, so I started asking her questions to figure out what she really wanted to know. During the course of our hour-long conversation, I learned that, ultimately, she was trying to make sense of her life. Her parents had divorced when she was young. She and her brother clung together through the difficult years that followed and tried to cope with new stepparents and stepsiblings on both sides. Her father threw himself into what she called his "new family." Her mother was devastated by the divorce and constantly complained about her father. That put her in the middle and made her the emotional caretaker of her mom, and her brother the referee of their parents' ongoing conflict. Meanwhile, she never knew what to do with her two stepparents and found the relationships taxing at best. Neither parent, nor stepparent, was safe or available to her.

Her question about "psychological issues" and being from a blended family was really about her; she was trying to figure out how to cope with the residue of her complex family. While the wording of her question surprised me, her fundamental journey did not; I meet a lot of young adults with the same pressing question.

It was obvious to me that her parents and stepparents had very little insight into how their behavior and choices affected her well-being. I find that, despite their good intentions, this is often true of parents and stepparents. My stepfamily counseling and coaching experience of more than twenty-five years confirms that most don't really understand what it is to be a child of divorce living in a stepfamily, nor how this affects how children respond to parenting. Stepparents, in particular, who lack a child-informed perspective on their role find themselves struggling to connect and lead. On the other hand, stepparents who do empathize well parent more wisely, compassionately, and effectively, and find that their blended family is more likely to thrive.

That's why I personally pursued the publication of this book. You can either come alongside your children and help them heal and find love and emotional safety—and in the process, also strengthen your home—or you can inadvertently add to their "psychological issues." Lauren helps capture the journey of stepparenting firsthand, from a stepchild's perspective. *In Their Shoes* helps you find empathy for the child(ren) in your life and empowers you to do the former rather than the latter.

—Ron L. Deal, bestselling author of a series of books for
blended families including *The Smart Stepfamily*,
and consulting editor of the SMART STEPFAMILY Series

Introduction

Every so often a conversation stops you in your tracks and leaves an indelible mark on your spirit. These sentiments turn moments into movements, challenge growth, and ultimately refine our character.

Last summer, a group of friends decided to connect weekly around a table filled with delicious food and directed dialogue. One of our guests was pregnant for the duration of our gatherings, and as her due date approached, she expressed her anticipated joy with great enthusiasm. For my friend Kayla, this season came with great expectations. Kayla was about to experience the miracle of birth. This would be her first biological child, but not her first time in the role of a mother. She is a stepmom. Her husband had a son from a previous relationship—a young boy she had embraced with open arms from the moment they met.

Becoming a stepmom had its challenges, and for Kayla something felt extra challenging about welcoming a biological child into the blended family. When we asked her about how she was processing the transition, she said, "I've accepted that this [being a stepmom] will hurt a little bit, every day, forever." She further explained, "Allowing myself to accept the imperfections and struggles makes the journey much easier."

Kayla felt exhausted trying to navigate her role with perfection, and she recognized that owning the hard parts made her blended family experience better. Accepting the routine pain-points she felt—and knew she would continue to feel—brought freedom where she previously felt captive.

I will always remember her words: Being a stepparent can hurt a little bit, every day, forever. It may never feel perfect, but it will be purposeful. You are sure to experience a roller coaster of emotions as you strive to connect with the children in your new role. When the feelings you experience are hurt feelings, try not to internalize them as your failures. Seeking perfection will exhaust you and will often leave you feeling disappointed. I know that I was the cause of many of my stepparents' hurt feelings. My conversation with Kayla triggered some of my own family memories, and I wanted her to know that eventually some of the pain would dissipate.

I told Kayla that it was going to be okay—that light would follow the darkness. She was doing an incredible job, and ultimately was not alone. I did my best to share some of the emotions I felt as a stepchild and asked her to trust that the hard was not her fault. Divorce comes with pain-points: Parents feel them, stepparents feel them, and children feel them. We seek to find fault in people, or in roles, but there is no universal truth for casting blame.

"Thanks for the helpful perspective," Kayla said after my offered encouragement. "You should write it down." Her suggestions met with a few additional promptings to capture my sentiments on paper and to potentially use some of my story to encourage and help other blended families better understand the experience from a child's perspective. Maybe these stories could assuage some of the unintended hurt other families might be struggling to navigate.

This idea planted a seed in my heart to dream about the possibility of writing a book. I never could have imagined that this dream would quickly become a reality.

The Power of Empathy

In 2017 I was invited to speak at the FamilyLife Blended Summit in Nashville. I remember walking into an auditorium filled with more than five hundred leaders from around the globe, all leaning in to learn and bring hope to thousands of people who are categorized as blended families. I sat in one of the back rows, looked down at my name badge, and felt the power of these words from 2 Samuel 7:18 (NLT): "Who am I, O sovereign LORD, and what is my family, that you have brought me this far?" I felt overwhelmed with gratitude, as I was acutely aware that God was beginning in me something much bigger than myself.

How am I the one sitting in this chair right now? What do I have to share that can make any difference? Countless children have experienced growing up in a post-divorce blended family setting and, somehow, I had been given a platform to talk about it. After experiencing an incredible sense of awe, I began to feel a big wave of responsibility. Families were longing to bring something home with them that might help. They were eager for resources and tools that might make a difference. In my experience with relationships, one of the most powerful skills in working toward healing is empathy. Empathy allows a chance for each person to see another perspective and often aids in building a bridge toward understanding and compassion.

These sentiments are an imperative part of the blended family experience. Most people who walk through the process of two families merging post-divorce feel dissonance, and often hurt, in the journey. Looking at the blended experience through a lens that is layered in pain lends itself to defenses and division rather than approachability and appreciation.

When people not only hear someone else's perspective but also feel it, reconciliation has a chance. There are so many dynamics to explore as families strive to blend in a healthy way. My hope is to share some of the missing data points and information that children rarely can communicate while they are in the throes of childhood and adolescence.

Both biological parents and stepparents will benefit from approaching common struggles with new information regarding the child's perspective. In either role, new perspective may bring clarity and awareness to the sometimes-bewildering posture of a child's post-divorce attitude. Whether you are the biological parent or the stepparent in your blended family, my hope is that as you digest the words on these pages, you would feel encouraged, validated, and optimistic. May you better understand, with new perspective, life in your family through a child's eyes.

A Note to My Own Stepparents

As a stepchild myself, I fully recognize that my attitude, words, and posture were (and sometimes still are) a source of hurt for my stepparents. To both of you, I want to say, "Thank you."

Thank you for embracing me with love, even when my attitude was less than lovely. Thank you for being patient with my process as I regularly challenged your pursuits. Thank you for showing up, even when I acted like I did not want you around. Thank you for giving me grace when I didn't deserve it. Adjusting to our new lives together did not come with an instruction manual, and more than likely, if it had, I probably would not have followed the rules. We have been through a lot together. You have watched me grow. You have helped me grow, and now you are helping my children grow.

My children will never know you as stepgrandparents because you have fully embraced them as your own. Watching you invest in their lives brings me unspeakable joy. Please know you play a vital role in their lives. As my parents' spouses, you have been faithful and loyal through some very trying circumstances. I appreciate the way you have modeled steadfast commitment, honoring your vows even when it has been hard.

May the words on these pages give both of you a better understanding of the emotional process I experienced as a child. I hope you find clarity in misunderstanding and continued healing in the hurt. Both of you mean a lot to me. I am humbled and thankful for the role you play in my life. Thank you for your steadfast endurance to continue leaning in, learning, and loving. I see you. I love you. You matter. Take heart, our best is yet to come.

1

A Family Designation

God's infallible character always weaves a redemptive storyline for those who trust in Him, yet redemption is impossible without fully understanding and facing the pain of the cross.

I have always loved words. They have meaning, depth, power, and influence. I attribute my passion for language to the dedicated efforts of my parents and the intentional ways they integrated vocabulary lessons into many childhood road-trip adventures.

With four kids in our family, driving was a necessity for travel. College savings accounts seemed like a better investment than plane tickets for six. For many families, when road trips come to mind, they reminisce about the alphabet game, the license plate challenge, or a billboard scavenger hunt. In my family, however, the first memory associated with cross-country travel is the dictionary. Merriam-Webster typically rode shotgun in our baby-blue hatchback station wagon. Our parents would take turns reading a word and casting the spotlight on one of their children to guess its meaning and, for bonus points, apply it in a sentence.

Naturally, we were competitive and wanted to correctly identify definitions. This meant points for our individual egos and affirmation from our doting parents. One summer, en route to the Grand Canyon, my younger brother pulled ahead with big points on his dictionary scoreboard. "Okay," my mom set the stage, "your word is apathy."

"I. Don't. Care!" My brother scoffed as he rolled his eyes, annoyed by a game he did not consider fun.

"That's right!" My parents celebrated. "That's exactly what apathy means." As young kids, we rarely appreciated this intentional effort to expand our vocabulary and understanding of language. Now, as an adult in the communication field, I couldn't be more grateful for the discipline to understand and communicate using words that have depth, meaning, and influence. There is no shortage of words to describe my family growing up.

Adventurous, Athletic, and Altruistic

We explored the landscape of our home in the foothills, adopting wild garter snakes as pets and building snow tunnels to our neighbor's house. We camped on the sandy beaches of Lake McConaughy and navigated rental RVs across the national landscape. Summers led us on a quest for blue ribbons in our swim meets, while focused discipline refined our skills enough to attempt a junior golf championship. With each season change, our athletic endeavors took a new shape. Winters we welcomed ski season, when we tackled challenging mogul runs, and as they melted into spring, we grabbed shin guards and cleats to fulfill the suburban soccer mom dream.

Our family valued faith and modeled what it meant to put others first and contribute to those in need. Sometimes we took it to the extreme, or Xtremes, which was the name we chose for our family keyboard and drum band. Our church hosted a fundraiser for kids with special needs and sold tickets to an Xtremes concert, fully benefiting the cause. We rocked the stage, covering artists such as Madonna and the Beatles, and we even got a shot at merchandizing by selling originally designed band T-shirts to adoring fans.

Boisterous, Brave, and Bookish

With four children born within a span of six years, our family was quite visible in our small mountain community. Our Italian and German heritage didn't aid attempts to blend in and stay quiet. We left a mark at our elementary school, following one after the other, and leaving teachers eager to receive our last name on the next year's roster. Our house was rarely empty, bustling with people and energy. Birthday parties, team pep rallies, and holiday reunions left echoes of joy in our home each year. Take risks, dream big, aim high. These mantras set the tone to face judges for a shot at landing a lead role on stage, break bones in a banana-board race down our steep mountain driveway, or keep a death grip on the hammock as siblings flipped one another 180 degrees over a sharp rock landing.

Our shenanigans, considered brave by some and stupid by others, were balanced with a strict family value to engage the brain. Be smart, work hard, pursue excellence, and make good grades. The honor roll was familiar territory for our namesake. As sons and daughters of a surgeon and registered nurse, we strove to make Dad and Mom proud. Academic achievement was highly valued, and we felt celebrated when reaching our goals with an abundance of love and support.

Courteous, Communal, and Christian

Manners mattered big-time in our family. When we were being directed by an authority figure, "Yes, sir" and "Yes, ma'am" were the nonnegotiable responses. Mom taught a manners-and-etiquette class at our elementary school and enrolled each of us to join her roster. The expectations were clear: Put others first, hold doors open, respect your elders, and don't smack your lips. These character qualities weren't commanded—they were modeled. Our parents were polite, kind, and very well respected in our community. Extended family lived far away and only flew in for the big holidays. Visitors were common over Christmas, but rarely did out-of-town family jet-set for Easter or birthdays.

Although geographic distance left gaps between family visits, friends were always present. We lived within a community where the titles of Aunt and Uncle were not limited to relatives, but rather became an endearing moniker for countless adults in our lives. Mom wore multiple hats, serving as the PTA president and regional coordinator for MOPS (Mothers of Preschoolers) and CBS (Community Bible Study). We lived in a place where, truly, everyone knows your name.

Our family felt most connected at church—a church that began as a small-group Bible study in my parents' living room years before. We served together alongside people who fell in love with Jesus and had a passion to plant a church and reach others with truth. I remember flipping through the blue binder of worship songs placed on folding chairs in an elementary school gym and raising my hand to request a song.

"Can we please sing 'Amazing Grace'?"

"Sure thing, Lauren." As the guitar chords began, I excitedly positioned my heart for worship. God was alive in our family and meant everything to my parents, who both came to know Him as college students, led by friends and mentors who broke the religious mold and shared the experience of life transformed through personal relationship. Loving God mattered in our family and assured us of His power and His presence in all circumstances.

Dubious, Discouraged, and Divorced

The first signs of discord hit when I entered middle school. Dad's lengthy work commute became difficult to manage, so my parents advocated a move closer to the hospital. Our roots were deep in our quaint foothills town, yet the appeal of living five minutes from Dad's office was alluring. His hours were demanding, and valuable time spent with him meant everything. The move played to our family's adventurous spirit.

"We're going to buy some land, which means we get to build our very own house from scratch," Mom informed us. "You'll get to choose your rooms, and we'll have space to play games in the yard and maybe even get a dog!" What kids don't love the puppy promise? Transition was hard, but saying good-bye paved the way for a brighter future being closer as a family and attending bigger schools with access to more opportunities. We settled in to the new digs and found a great rhythm. Our setting changed, but our family remained healthy—or so I thought.

Family meetings were a regular occurrence in our upbringing, but rarely were they scheduled while on vacation. Something was wrong. As Dad called the four of us kids into the living area, we could see the physical and emotional distance between our parents. Mom sat across the room—a somber, serious tone replacing her normally effervescent demeanor. The announcement was quick, to the point, and very matter-of-fact.

"Your mom and I haven't been happy for a while, and I've decided to move out of the house."

Haven't been happy? I thought, bewildered and confused. *We just had an incredible day skiing together; everyone is happy. What do you even mean?* Emotions exploded in different directions. Each family member responded to what they heard with their own coping mechanism. Some sought escape and left the condo to avoid the reality of what had just transpired.

I remember seeking refuge under a large down comforter, hoping that maybe disappearing and hiding would change the reality of what had just occurred. That comforter absorbed many salty tears that wouldn't subside. *This is not happening. This can't be real.* I closed my eyes, exhausted from the emotional weight. I woke up to a new reality. My family would never be the same.

This ski weekend marked the beginning of a long season of counseling efforts to restore what had broken. Just a few years later, as a sophomore in high school, I became a child of divorce. Divorce was now the defining characteristic of our family.

Wasn't this supposed to happen to other families—to dysfunctional families, to lost families, to families who fought and yelled, families with serious issues? Doubt permeated my spirit. *This cannot be real. There is still time to change things. Something will renew my hope in this time of great discouragement.* However, no amount of effort, faith, or energy would change my forever family. Our family was now a statistic on the losing side of marriage. My parents were divorced, and there was nothing I could do to change it.

According to the data, my new reality was supposed to be normal. I, like many teenagers, was privy to statistics supporting divorce as a common family structure. Adults approached us with motivating sound bites:

"Don't worry, kids are resilient."

"I know this is hard right now, but everyone will be happier and better off in the end."

"It will take a little getting used to, but this is good for your family."

These statements did not bring peace, and many of them felt contrary to what I was experiencing. In my circle of friends, no one had parents going through a divorce. Many of these parents were happily married, with no indication that anything could ever change that truth. None of my friends shuffled between houses and lost track of which contained their favorite pair of shoes. No one shared stories of packing a weekly suitcase for transport according to the 50/50 custody agreement.

And while many of the families in my circle were still part of intact marriages, most of them did not share my faith. I remember looking for signs to explain why our seemingly healthy family was suddenly falling apart after eighteen years of marriage, especially when the God I was seeking to understand was not appearing to be big enough to reconcile my parents' differences.

Grief, Fast-Forwarded

The sudden shift that children experience in the face of divorce feels jolting and confusing. Their loss is significant and their grief is heavy, yet the mindset and messages following the event are sometimes misguided or misleading. Divorce is lauded by some people as a courageous choice to find what makes someone happier. Others try to make it sound normal in conversation, as a healthy and justified option if a marriage is not panning out as it should.

Children are given a lot of credit in their role after a divorce. They are quickly labeled as resilient and malleable, adaptable and strong. They do possess the ability to overcome obstacles, yet the prevalence of well-intentioned, optimistic sound bites can minimize the depth of grief and loss children experience post-divorce. This creates pressure to move on without the necessary social supports required to fully address the pain. Often in the faith community, rushing the grief timeline seems to be supported with spiritual taglines: *God has a plan. God wouldn't give you more than you can handle.* God's infallible character always weaves a redemptive storyline for those who trust in Him, yet redemption is impossible without fully understanding and facing the pain of the cross.

This book is intended to help parents and stepparents see through a child's eyes some of the pain-points felt after divorce and to give voice to a child's process when assimilating to blended family dynamics. One of the most important things to recognize when entering the life of a child post-divorce is that each child, regardless of his or her family's circumstances, experiences one or more of the five stages of grief explored below. How children grieve is not universal, but what they grieve is.

Divorce is a painful reality for all involved. If you are anything like me, it sometimes feels easier to avoid the pain, yet doing so simply delays the healing process. I remember so desperately wanting to just get over it—to stop allowing our family's story to hurt. Somewhere along the way, my goal changed from getting over the divorce to getting through it. To do so, I had to embrace the grief.

It is important for parents, stepparents, and others in socially supportive roles to not only acknowledge the reality of grief post-divorce, but to also allow the emotional freedom for children to fully experience it. Minimizing grief after divorce can stifle their healing and emotional development, and rushing grief can unintentionally extend its timeline. As you encounter children who are experiencing, or have experienced, divorce as part of their story, remember the following stages of grief and how they may be contributing to the relationship dynamics between you.

Stage 1: Denial

The first stage of grief is denial, which is refusing to believe the reality of your situation. Many children cling to a subconscious hope that the divorce will not last forever and that someday their parents might realize they still love one another and reconcile. Kids visualize a happy ending and fill their minds with hopeful thoughts: *This isn't going to be the end of our family's story. Someday my parents will realize that this is not the right decision, or someone will talk some sense into them, and they'll eventually make up.* Hope is always a permissible mindset for children, and sometimes serves as one of their healthiest coping strategies. However, what they hope for rarely aligns with their future reality.

The movie *The Parent Trap* plays on this emotional narrative. In the film, a couple decides to divorce after having identical twin daughters. They each take a daughter; one lives with their mother in London, the other with their father in California. During a chance encounter at a summer camp that both twins *just happen* to attend, the girls simultaneously recognize their identical characteristics and discover they are sisters. Each pulls from her suitcase half of a photo that has been torn down the middle and realizes that they are twins. The rest of the summer, the girls plot and then switch roles, leaving camp with the opposite parent. They arrange a master plan to get their mom and dad in the same place and re-create their first date. The parents fall in love again and reunite as one happy family. Although this makes for a heartwarming movie ending, the storyline is misleading. Its message communicates that couples can easily be put in settings where they will remember their initial love story and be reminded of why they still belong together, but it creates an illusion of hope that rarely plays out in real life.

Nancy Kalish is a research professor at California State University and sought to determine the frequency of reconciled marriages post-divorce. A *Chicago Tribune* article, "Same Marriage, Round 2," tells us: "In her study of 1,001 reunited couples from around the world, only about 6 percent said they married, divorced and remarried the same person."[1]

The article continues to share supporting data from divorce cases managed by Philadelphia attorney David Steerman, who "recalls 'four or five' such reunions in the last 12 years of his high-volume practice. 'The more common result is once divorced, they stay divorced, but there are those exceptional couples who figure out how to make it back to one another,' he says."[2]

A couple's decision to divorce is rarely a haphazard or flippant choice. Both people often care deeply about their family and even still care about one another but, after exhausting efforts to save the marriage, conclude that divorce is their only option. Pain is a part of every marital dissolution no matter how amicable the split. Therefore, it is rare to see couples change their minds once a divorce is finalized. Reconciliation does happen, but it is not the norm. Even if children understand the finality of the decision, most experience a period of denial that leads to thoughts of a *Parent Trap*–like happy ending.

Stage 2: Anger

Children commonly experience anger as part of their grieving process. In the case of divorce, kids absorb a lifetime of this decision's consequences through no fault of their own. It feels unfair. Anger is a natural human response to an unjust situation. A child might think, *Why does my life have to be turned upside down because you two don't get along anymore?* Or, *Who gives you the right to dictate what happens to our family without even considering how it affects us?* Their anger feels justified. When parents split, each adult has the chance to close the door on the old and work toward their new. Any type of custody arrangement prevents the children from having this same right. For the rest of their lives, the children will split their lives, time, residences, and routines. If sole custody is granted to one parent, children may feel robbed of their right to relationship with the other.

Anger manifests in a variety of ways. A typically compliant child might rebel against house rules, or a normally easygoing child might begin throwing epic tantrums. These meltdown moments give children a sense of power as they process the anger they are feeling in a very powerless situation.

Stage 3: Bargaining

Next comes bargaining. For me, the evidence of this grief stage is written on the pages of my old journals: "Please God, help my parents fix this. You are big enough to change this story. The Bible says all things are possible with you, and you are in charge of my family. Please, please, help!"

Bargaining may be directed toward God, but it also happens between parent and child. Children may plead with one or both parents to change their minds. They may melt down during a custody rotation, holding one parent's leg as if they are not ready to part for a first day of preschool, or exit when a baby-sitter arrives. These behaviors are indicative of bargaining and are often a child's way of negotiating a situation that is fully out of their control. During this grief stage, children wrestle for a say in the outcome. Eventually, they recognize that nothing they do can or will change their parents' decision to divorce. As new routines and patterns form, new homes are set up, new schools are attended, and a new life begins to take shape, the energy required to continue to plead for change fizzles, and bargaining efforts fade. Sometimes, what follows their exhausted efforts is depression.

Stage 4: Depression

Depression does not discriminate and can affect both young children and adolescents. Its symptoms play out in a variety of ways and are not always easy to recognize. The American Academy of Child and Adolescent Psychiatry reports:

> The behavior of depressed children and teenagers may differ from the behavior of depressed adults. Child and adolescent psychiatrists advise parents to be aware of signs of depression in their youngsters. Consider seeking help if you observe:
>
> - Frequent sadness, tearfulness, crying
> - Decreased interest in or enjoyment of favorite activities
> - Hopelessness
> - Persistent boredom; low energy
> - Social isolation such as withdrawing from friends and family
> - Low self-esteem and guilt

- Extreme sensitivity to rejection or failure
- Increased irritability, anger, or hostility
- Difficulty with relationships
- Frequent complaints of physical illnesses such as head-aches and stomachaches
- Frequent absences from school or poor performance in school
- Poor concentration
- A major change in eating and/or sleeping patterns
- Talk of or efforts to run away from home
- Thoughts or expressions of suicide or self-destructive behavior[3]

Sometimes, children of divorce kick into extreme perfor-mance mode, attempting to mask their feelings to prove that they are okay. This pattern can lead to what is called extreme performance anxiety. Children suffering from extreme per-formance anxiety may appear to be doing even better after a divorce than they were beforehand. Emotionally, however, many who mask their grief in this way will eventually wear out and be vulnerable to an emotional crash.

This is how I dealt with divorce. I masked my sadness with busyness and performance. Determined not to let anyone see me as a statistic and not to succumb to the data-driven risk factors following divorce, I shifted into "prove them wrong" mode. I was not going to be one of the kids who turned to substances to cope; I wanted to demonstrate my strength by proving myself worthy of the moral high ground. Many stud-ies affirm that after a divorce, grades drop because students have difficulty focusing in class. Coaches report their athletes are distracted and do not give 100 percent on the field. As a fiercely competitive person, and someone who was hungry to prove that nothing could affect me, I overcompensated with a performance-based mentality and was determined not to let anyone see divorce having any negative impact on my life. I played harder, practiced longer, and pushed through athletic pursuits. Academically, I kicked my already high-achieving drive into overtime and graduated with straight A's in every class. I poured myself into friendships and spent time around their dinner tables rather than be stuck in the fragmented stories around my own. I was exhausted; I was in pain, but I was not going to let anyone know it.

Stage 5: Acceptance

Acceptance commonly is the final stage of the grieving cycle. Getting to this stage does not mean that children fully embrace divorce as right or okay, but they do come to terms with it being a reality in their family's story. Children in this stage of grief may begin to soften toward their parents and even express empathy or understanding for why divorce happened. They begin to look at their circumstance from a more positive perspective and may finally begin to pursue their own resources for help. Although there is no exact science determining a timeline for arriving at the acceptance stage, this season rarely happens quickly. For some, accepting the divorce narrative may not happen until a child leaves the home. For others, it happens as children grow into adolescence. Some may never be able to fully accept the reality of their family situation, while others might not only accept divorce, but will also be grateful that it happened.

There is no formula to normalize the grief process or timeline for every child of divorce. Some may move through the stages quickly; for others it may take literally a lifetime. Regardless of the timing, the effect of divorce is universal. According to

KidsHealth.org, "Every divorce will affect the kids involved—and many times the initial reaction is one of shock, sadness, frustration, anger, or worry. But kids also can come out of it better able to cope with stress, and many become more flexible, tolerant young adults."[4]

The next time you encounter behavior from a child or step-child that appears selfish, disrespectful, unkind, hurtful, or flat-out mean, consider their circumstances, and try to approach them with this new perspective. Many of the hurtful attitudes and behaviors exhibited in these relationships are not character flaws or personality faults, but rather they are a direct mani-festation of a child's grieving heart.

CHAPTER 1
TAKEAWAY SUMMARY

1. Look into the pre-divorce narrative of each side of your family before your blending-family process began. Consider the healthy functions that existed as a way to better understand the shock or sadness children are processing. Acknowledge that not all ele-ments in a pre-divorce story are negative. This might help culti-vate empathy when children struggle in accepting their blended family as "better" than their previous one.

2. Review the five stages of grief: denial, anger, bargaining, depres-sion, and acceptance. Assessing each child's process with its own unique experience, order, and timeline might help cultivate a better understanding of the difficult behavior patterns commonly exhibited in children after their parents divorce.

2

Power Play

With a single parent, children don't share the spotlight. Kids are prioritized as number one. When dating begins, and romantic feelings begin
to develop for a new person, priorities shift. Children feel like the shade
instead of the sun.

The power of advertising is real. My children have never
been to Arby's, yet during one of their recent adventures
in play, they were dressed up in ninja gear, shouting, "We have
the meat!" in deep, grown-up voices. Another time, I walked
past my daughter's door and she was humming a song. She has
a lovely voice, and I wanted to hear more of her joyful chorus.
I entered her room and asked her if she would be willing to
sing her song again. Expecting the latest Kidz Bop chorus or
a current billboard hit, I was surprised when she cleared her
throat, and sang, "Nationwide is on your side."

At first I laughed, but then I worried that our parenting was
flawed. Why are our children walking through the house reciting

marketing jingles? We don't watch *that* much TV; we don't even have cable. It is interesting how quickly those catchy jingles take root in our brains and trick us into thinking we need these products for our survival. As I look back on my childhood, I still can remember advertising jingles that have not aired in more than twenty years. The ones touting toys and candy were most likely to stick. The messages partnering advertising slogans are memorable and convincing. They become a refrain in our minds that prompt us to desire whatever is being sold. One such chorus from my childhood aimed to sell the powerful refreshment of Wrigley's Doublemint gum. The commercial featured images of twins chewing gum and having twice as much fun as everyone not indulging in the minty treat—doubling their pleasure and their fun with Doublemint gum, as the jingle urged.

There are a lot of positive connotations around the idea of doubling anything. A double scoop of ice cream is always more desirable than its single counterpoint. Doubling your money on an investment is a thrilling financial experience. Double-decker buses attract crowds from around the globe who are eager to catch a ride on a vehicle with two levels and an open-air top.

Although there are quite a few popular sentiments around the idea of doubling, there are some contexts in which people try to avoid duplication. When enjoying your favorite Mexican restaurant, you rarely welcome a table of double-dippers around the chips and salsa. When taxes double, no one is ready to celebrate with high fives and confetti poppers. When a teacher doubles the amount of homework assigned, students do not line up in front of the classroom to say thank you. Most people are eager to accept the rewards in duplication. Many, however, are more hesitant when double means trouble.

Divorce comes with a doubling effect. Although there are known hurts that accompany a divided family, sometimes the duplicated nature of life for kids after divorce is spun from a posture of excitement. People begin to say things like, "Now you get to have two of everything—double the birthday presents, double the holiday celebrations, and two different bedrooms." In my experience, I remember some of my friends expressing jealousy over my access to two of everything. Although the duplicity factor does sound intriguing, the perks feel short-lived. Children do not want to live a double life. After a divorce, two does not always feel better than one.

Living Single

Before divorce, children see two people living as one flesh through marriage. Children typically do not see the "single" season of their parents' lives. Granted, there are times when one parent is alone while the other is working or traveling, yet each day (or trip) ends with both parents under one roof. After divorce, unless a parent has already established a new romantic relationship, time spent with parents is almost exclusively in settings where they are alone. Each home or apartment is decorated with one style and only some of the furnishings that used to occupy the corners of a previous residence. Dinner menus and recipes change as both parents learn a new rhythm in the kitchen. There are different routines for laundry, different days for trash pickup, and different addresses to fill out on school paperwork. Formerly divided roles are no longer split. Both parents grocery shop, both cook, both clean, both mow the lawn, both manage the money, and both decorate.

Watching this transition is often a strange experience for children. As they observe their parents' roles shift, they struggle to know their own role. Every previous pattern takes on a new setting, and a reset button is pressed to help begin making sense of the new world around them. Although the settings, roles, and patterns change, the personalities of each parent tend to remain the same. Even though one may be spending more time in the kitchen and one more time with the bank statements, both still resemble being themselves, just in a different setting. Children find peace knowing that they can expect to see an authentic representation of Mom or Dad, even if they now live in different houses. It takes time to adjust to the new rhythms in each home. Children begin to embrace the patterns of their parents' single lives. If a dating relationship starts, patterns change yet again. This shift requires children to adapt to a third set of expectations, which can heighten emotional stress.

Dating Jitters

There is something very special about the post-college roommate season. For me, this life stage was spent with three of my closest friends in a charming ranch-style house near our former college campus. Our front-porch swing became the setting for cherished conversations about life-altering decisions. One such decision was marked with great anticipation yet equally met with pressure and fear: What rattled our hearts more than anything was when we began a new dating relationship. Dating is exciting, yet it comes with its own set of nerve-racking moments.

Living in community during many of our first serious dating pursuits was fun. Sometimes we got to be in the background for the first phone call. A cell phone would chime, and squeals of excitement were hushed with the wave of a hand and a finger pressed to pursed lips.

"Hello," a roommate answers, faking a calm and collected composure. The rest of us hear only her responses, huddling while eagerly awaiting the hang-up to process the conversation. "I'd love to. See you then!" After a confirmed hang-up, we ask for the details. "What did he say?" "Where is he taking you?" "What will you wear?" Excitement permeates the atmosphere, and the preparations begin. The dating scene is fun, but the pressure and nerves that often accompany each outing can alter the patterns and behaviors of both participants. Stakes feel high. Each wants to put his or her best foot forward. We rush to clean the house, find the right outfit, wear the right hairstyle, and play the right role.

Watching these dating jitters play out with a single friend is fun and exciting. When the jitters are happening with a parent, the emotional reaction is not always as fun. A parent's desire to impress another person carries stress, and this pressure can be transmitted to the children.

Best Behavior

It is difficult to remember the details surrounding the onset of dating with each of my parents. Both sides experienced the stress of receiving my distant and moody response when introducing someone they were developing feelings for. I never decided to act standoffish or rude, but I believe my posture added even more stress to a situation that was already stressful for my parents. Although I cannot remember specific details about what I said or how I said it, I vividly recall the pep talks that ensued after a date's departure. When the door closed behind a potential new suitor, I would prepare to be questioned about why I had to make the process more difficult than it needed to be. "I get that this is hard for you," each would express. "But your attitude makes it even worse. This relationship is happening, and I need you to be nice."

Looking back, I fully recognize how difficult my pushback made dating for each of my parents, yet at the time, my actions were the only way I knew to cope. When parents begin dating after a divorce, children lose the emotional safety and autonomy in each home. As soon as each new house and routine begins to feel normal, strangers are introduced and disrupt the newfound rhythm. Both houses feel more like a stage for performing than a respite for relaxing. Children feel pressure to perform, always putting their best face forward without the freedom to take off masks and be themselves. This emotional process is draining. Sometimes it is partnered with guilt, because children recognize their parent's dissatisfaction with this disruptive posture as each begins dating.

Have you ever experienced a high-stakes job interview? Do you remember how you felt? If your experience was anything like mine, the emotional energy required to sustain the process felt draining. Before entering the interview setting, you most likely took one last peek in the mirror to adjust your hairstyle or to check your teeth for a poppy seed lingering after a breakfast bagel. You may have freshened your makeup or buttoned your sport coat, all while looking into the mirror, practicing your previously rehearsed handshake and hello. As you entered the scene, you held yourself with a confident posture and monitored your speech for nervous filler words that might poorly reflect on your otherwise proper and educated business acumen. Each question felt like an opportunity to share your best accomplishments, and even when discussing weaknesses, you had hope that your potential employer would see your capacity for resilience and strength.

You were full of grace and wit, dressed to impress, watchful, and intentional. As the interview neared its end, you communicated graciously and offered thanks for the opportunity. A final handshake and friendly salutation indicated the conversation was over. The exit brought great relief as you took one last deep breath and walked briskly to your car. Driving away, your spirit settled. You did it! You put your best foot forward and hopefully proved that you were the right candidate for the role. As you waited to hear their final decision, you probably felt a bit anxious. In the meantime, you took a deep breath and relaxed. The most difficult part was now behind you, and all you could do was wait.

This analogy helps explain how children feel when their parents transition from being single to starting a new relationship. Through a child's lens, however, the interview lasts much longer than an hour or two. A new person's presence changes the atmosphere; it becomes difficult to conduct daily routines authentically. Having a guard up takes energy, and as energy is exhausted, children are more susceptible to meltdowns and mood swings.

Picture the after-school attitudes parents routinely encounter. Sometimes the side of your children you see is the antithesis of what their teachers and friends experience. Helpful, kind, and gracious behaviors fail to make it home. Instead, you witness Oscar-worthy tantrums and attitudes you would not recognize in a normal, everyday setting. The *best behavior* pressure may play into the struggles potential stepparents feel from the very beginning. The stories their biological parent have shared with you do not always align with the actions and responses you feel from the child. If you encounter frustrating and hurtful behavior from children during your dating experience, do your best not to interpret it as a character issue. Extend grace to them in the same way you hope for grace from them.

Some of you may have experienced, or are now experiencing, the opposite of the behavior described above. Rather than offering you eye-rolls and disrespectful behaviors, it is very possible that the children add a warmth and depth to your dating journey that makes life even better. One stepmother I talked with shared that meeting the child and involving him in the dating scene was what convinced her that this relationship was *the one*. As we discussed the nerves and emotional experience of her first date, she recalled the respect she felt for her partner, who invited his son along to the ice cream parlor. "From the beginning," he began, as they waited in line to sample flavors, "I need you to know that this is what life looks like with me." Her response to this gesture was one of admiration and respect. She enjoyed the energy his son brought to each adventure, and she now had a little admirer and buddy who routinely filled her cup. The woman described herself in a fun "friend" or "baby-sitter" role during this time. "He lit up every time he saw me," she explained, "and he was very affectionate and affirming whenever I was around." For this family, dating was a bit of a honeymoon season. As our conversation continued, she explained that her struggles came later, after the couple married. We will explore this transition in the next chapter.

Demoted

Nothing quite prepares you for the challenges and rewards that come with parenting. Whether by birth, adoption, or a blend, assuming the role of parent humbles and shapes us like nothing else can. People prepare for their transition to parenthood in a variety of ways. Some empty library shelves of every advice book, making notes of the do's and don'ts to read and reread. Others embrace the adventure with a spontaneous wait-and-see mentality; with a hopeful and optimistic spirit, a learn-on-the-go mindset feels best. Some nest, some rest, yet all who embrace the adventure experience the family overhaul that happens after children.

Before children, couples sit at the top of their family organizational chart. As children enter the mix, couples quickly realize the temptation to shift priority and focus from a partner-first mentality to a child-first structure. As soon as a child wraps his or her tiny hands around your finger, it's easy to understand the temptation to consider a power shift in the family's structure.

My vocational experience serves as an ever-present reminder to intentionally fight for and prioritize marriage ahead of children. This conviction compelled me to speak this commitment out loud within minutes of holding my first child. When the nurses placed our firstborn daughter in my arms, I looked my husband in the eye and said, "You are still my number one." He kissed my forehead and smiled. Soon afterward, I interrupted with, "Although, she is a very close second!" We laughed and cried and embraced the intimacy in this milestone memory. The words I spoke were purposeful and required me to live my promise.

The reason I felt compelled to speak this sentiment out loud was that without my husband and our marriage, this child would not be here. My love for him came before my love for my daughter, and to protect this baby's family legacy, I knew I had to honor a family structure where Dad came before daughter. My children are absolutely a priority, but they are third in line when it comes to vested relational energy. God has ultimate priority; my husband, Josh, comes next; and then my children. Owning my sentiment meant that I would work to continue investing energy in learning and meeting his needs, even when a completely dependent newborn had stolen our hearts. This partner-first mentality continues to be one we work on as a team, and sometimes our children compete to keep us from modeling it in our everyday actions.

Marriage helps keep the partner-before-child structure functioning, but after a divorce, children naturally fit into the previously prioritized partner's role. One-on-one time with each parent in custody-sharing arrangements allows a new and strong bond to form. This newfound one-on-one parental attention becomes a helpful coping mechanism as children process the hurt. It helps to shine positive light during a difficult season. Kids might think, *Dad and Mom may not be together anymore, but at least when I get to see each of them, they give me their undivided love and attention.*

For me, this season brought a lot of healing. I traveled with just my dad and had the chance to make memories that were only ours to treasure. My mom and I strengthened our relationship through shared grief and empathy. Even though my parents were no longer together, it was clear that they still loved me, and I still felt safe and known in their newfound single-parent rhythm.

With a single parent, children don't share the spotlight. Kids are prioritized as number one. But when dating begins and romantic feelings begin to develop for a new person, priorities shift. Children feel as though they are the shade instead of the sun. This process is not always met with warmth and understanding. After parents and children have worked to establish confidence in a family routine, a new person enters the scene; children feel demoted and attempt to reclaim their newfound position of power. The one-on-one parenting structure changes to a two-versus-one scenario. To combat the change, children adopt a defensive posture and fight to maintain their power. When this happens, the dating adults are vulnerable to becoming targets for rude behavior and interpersonal attacks.

Power Play

In seventh grade my friend invited me to join her family at the inaugural home opener for the Colorado Avalanche. I had never seen an NHL hockey game before and was bubbling over with questions about the rules. The stadium was full of electricity as Denver fans embraced their newest professional sports team. With each check, the plexiglass shook, and after a fight broke out on the ice, red lights spun on the scoreboard with sirens indicating an exciting development. A lit graphic bounced to the center of the screen, and the sportscaster bellowed, "It's time for an Avalanche power play!"

"What's a power play?" I asked my friend's dad.

He explained that a power play happens when a penalty takes one team's player off the ice, so the other team gets two minutes to try to score a goal with one extra person playing offense. Basically, it gives one team a huge advantage to get to the net, he said. Intrigued, I stood to join the rest of the fans in amplified cheering to encourage a goal. During a power play, the offensive team maintains the momentum. The other team shifts to a strictly defensive posture and aims to keep the opponent from scoring. The power play is intentionally designed to give one team an advantage. This metaphor explains a similar power play that transpires among children when their mom or dad's new boyfriend or girlfriend enters the mix. The family structure no longer involves a *just the two of us* culture. Instead, there are two adults paired on a team, and they seem to steal the relationship momentum from the parent-child routine. Mom or Dad is now acutely focused on someone else. Their energy and time are suddenly split. When children recognize the momentum shift, defenses go up to protect the home team's net.

Look back to the hockey power-play analogy. When one team suddenly has a man-up advantage, the opposing team's defense kicks into overdrive. If the offensive team scores within the allotted time frame, a huge celebration ensues. Chest bumps, hockey stick high fives, and fan cheers permeate the stadium. These are the moments that bond a team like nothing else can. They get a taste of victory together, and that victory unites the players and makes them feel closer to one another. Children are leery of these celebratory bonding victories in a parent's dating relationship because they signify that there is a great chance this team will stick together. If their parent does end up bonding with a new person, it likely signifies that parent will never bond again with their former spouse. When dating relationships get serious, a child's dream of his or her parents reconciling dies, and with that death may come a second round of post-divorce grief.

Full Season Perspective

The time people spend in dating relationships normally is shorter than the period they spend being single or remarried. Be encouraged, knowing that the dynamics in this stage truly last for but a short season of your life. When rooting for your home team, it is perfectly normal to hope for more wins than losses. I rarely have met a fan who hopes that his team will come home on the losing end, yet when it happens, committed fans do not allow themselves to lose heart. The next game will offer a fresh start and another chance to fight for that W.

Biological parents who begin dating after a divorce sometimes express that their kids make them feel like they are losing. If you find yourself in a similar place, take courage and know that this is just a season. Celebrate small victories, and try not to let the losses fully deflate your spirit. Remind yourself that for many children, this season is one in which all defenses are engaged. It is a child's last chance to assert power to try to change the outcome of the divorce. Emotionally, they are still adjusting to a new setting. Like a player drafted after many seasons in one place, they are learning what life looks like wearing a new jersey, in a new stadium, with new players. Children struggle, holding on to past loyalties that are difficult to break. It is extremely challenging for them to begin rooting for a team they have never seen play.

Remember that every season provides opportunities for growth. During losing seasons, committed fans stay loyal and cheer for the players while they work to overcome their mistakes. Winning seasons bring entire communities together to celebrate and affirm the victories. Wherever you find yourself in the process, remember that the dating season does not last forever, and eventually, if you choose to commit to a new team, you are sure to experience some wins along the way.

CHAPTER 2
TAKEAWAY SUMMARY

1. If you are beginning a dating relationship post-divorce, remember that children have recently invested a lot of emotional energy to accept their parent's new role as single.

2. When dating begins, another adaptation season begins in a child's life. Remember to allow space for this transition, and approach it with empathy.

3. Children feel a lot of pressure to perform and be on their best behavior in front of people who begin dating relationships with

their parents. Recognize that this process drains them emotionally and often triggers meltdowns and/or grumpy behavior.

4. Recognize that prior to your involvement in dating, the children have most likely become the top priority for each parent post-divorce. As parents begin to prioritize dating, children tend to feel demoted and seek opportunities for reclaiming some of their lost power.

5. The one-on-one relationship with their parent that children become accustomed to after divorce changes into a power-play setup when another adult enters the picture. This often heightens children's defenses and can feel like an attack.

6. Trust that dating only lasts for a season. Having a long-term future mindset may help lessen the pain of the individual attacks along the way. Also, remember that committing to a team means you must accept both the moments that feel like a win as well as those that bring feelings of loss and defeat.

3

Remembering Their Vows

When a new marriage takes place, the original pieces of life before divorce quickly evaporate. A brand-new stage is set, while the heart of the child is often longing for the original script.

Our family loves a tradition we have adopted with our neighbors. Once a month, we rotate hosts and plan a meal. When it is our turn to host, we cover a cooler of boxed juice drinks and Colorado microbrews with ice. With the front door propped open, our kids stand guard at the window. "When are they coming?" they incessantly ask, with eyes peeled for the first family to arrive. Around the corner, they catch a glimpse of silver scooters carrying their friends. Adult footsteps follow, and voices shout, "They're here! They're here!" Within minutes, a quiet, orderly house transforms into a bustling scene of hellos, hugs, and hot pans. These gatherings are intended not only to share food but to share life. Nine kids clear their plates and disperse into the backyard. Creative conversations typically spawn new games. The group leaders bust inside and begin gathering supplies.

"Mom, we need a bucket, two Wiffle Balls, a jump rope, and a squirt gun."

"Help yourselves," I reply. "Just make sure no one gets hurt." As the adults peek through the window, we witness childhood at its best. We see the older kids explaining the rules and the youngest being shuffled into position on their teams. Everyone's involvement ensures time inside for the adults to converse about child-related topics.

One such conversation revealed the tension one parent felt after his daughter received an award during a swimming competition for finishing in eighth place: "Why would they give her an award? She was practically last. Kids need to learn that there are actual qualifications for winning. I wanted to take her ribbon away." Another couple echoed their frustration, explaining that their son had three chances to bring a grade up after performing poorly on a spelling test. Every family in attendance added to the dialogue, sparking a debate about the frustrations when children are rewarded for mediocre performance. We unanimously agreed that children need grace and deserve a fair shot at a second chance. On the other hand, there was equal sentiment affirming the value of allowing kids to experience the natural consequences of not meeting performance requirements. The fear of failure should never paralyze someone from taking new risks or attempting challenging tasks. Even the most skilled individuals sometimes take a loss.

Learning how to cope with loss is an invaluable life skill. Parents' hearts, however, are woven in a protective posture, ready to rescue kids from ever having to experience the emotions (and sometimes the consequences) of being on the losing side. When adults see their children strictly through this protective lens, they tend to soften the blow of a losing situation by calling it a win. This *everybody wins* mentality is not an accurate representation of a child's future life experiences.

Wins, Losses, and Weddings

Many of us have heard the popular quote, "It is not about winning or losing, but how you play the game." If this is the case, is it fair to respond with disappointment at a loss? And what about situations in which both teams deserve a win?

I remember sitting in the stands during our high school's state championship football game. The seniors were hungry for a win, knowing that a state title would leave a powerful legacy for the football program and the class of 2000. Our high school had more than four thousand students, and almost all of them were in the stands cheering that day.

The tension in this scene was that our opponent was Columbine High School. Just one year prior to this matchup, Columbine had become a household name after one of our nation's first school shootings. I will never forget the moment our student body learned the details and went home to process the tragic event. The news aired during my seventh-period biology class: *Breaking news—two Columbine High School students opened fire on campus today. Twelve students have died in addition to one faculty member. Many others have reported injuries and have been admitted at the local hospital.* The bell rang and students spilled into the hallways, devastated and distraught. We were heading home with a sense of stolen innocence and a fear unknown in our world prior to this unthinkable tragedy.

In the stands at the state football championship, there was no room for the usual unbridled rivalry. Compassion, grief, and gut-wrenching pain brought two sides together. Still, there was a competition to play out, and only one team would win. The nation had its eye on Columbine High School and rallied for a victory.

I felt torn. I knew some of the players on our team and what a win would mean to them. I wore our colors with pride and stood ready to celebrate each touchdown. Our players had not suffered like Columbine's had, but they had worked hard to get to this point and wanted to see their work pay off.

Our team pulled ahead early in the first quarter, and we felt confident about our chance of winning. But as I watched our points accumulate, my heart suddenly felt divided. A sense of guilt crept through my spirit as I thought about the pain endured by the other side. How could I root against them when they had been through so much hurt? How could I celebrate our team's successes, when the other side continued to live in defeat? I was loyal to my school. I had pride in the community and felt connected to my team. We knew one another. On the other side of the stadium sat strangers. Yet my heart shifted its loyalty, and I embraced the dreams of a team of strangers—students and families who I felt needed a win much more than we did.

At the beginning of the third quarter, my school's team had a commanding lead. But I felt a premonition that Columbine was going to make a comeback. So many people were rooting for them; for Columbine, it was much more than a football championship—victory would be symbolic of a new beginning for a community that had been so broken. We turned the ball over, and their quarterback took the snap, completing a long throw down the sidelines. The wide receiver made his way into the end zone, and the touchdown and extra point swung momentum in favor of our opponent. Columbine went on to defeat us with a national audience celebrating their win.

We felt the sting of disappointment throughout the stands, yet a part of everyone on our side felt thankful that Columbine won. They fought hard. They found victory after grief and celebrated as champions. Even though I felt compelled to celebrate with them, a part of me felt heavy and sad for our team's loss. My heart felt like it was in the middle of a tug-of-war. I had reason to root for a win on each side, but in the end, I continued to feel split.

These same torn feelings can manifest in children as they prepare to watch their parents remarry.

Weddings are occasions marked by love and joy. They are like the state championship of the dating season. Everything a couple works for in their relationship is preparation for the big event. It is their chance for a celebratory win and something that deserves devoted fan and family support. Children can share in this excitement and want their parents to have a second chance at a winning marriage; however, their countenance may not always communicate this sentiment.

The wedding day changes everything, and during the celebration, children internally process whether the changes will be for better or for worse. I remember preparing my heart to witness another person taking my parent's hand and exchanging vows. The emotional process felt like a wrestling match. One side of me was thankful to see each of my parents get a second chance at love, but the other side was cautious and scared about the reality of this change. I do not believe there is a universal emotional experience for children as they participate in a parent's wedding festivities. There are, however, some common themes that play out during the transition. The next sections outline some of the emotional processes observed in children and stepchildren, both during and after a post-divorce wedding day.

Processing Permanence

When exploring the topic of the wedding day with stepparents and stepchildren, I often hear, "The kids were all on board, and even excited, when we announced our engagement, but as the wedding day approached and the celebration ensued, it's like they totally changed and began pushing every one of our buttons. What is this all about?"

The wedding day is one of the first concrete symbols of permanent change that children must process. While biological parents are single or in the dating stage, space remains for autonomy and safety in the rhythms of their previous family's life. Sure, Mom or Dad may go out for dinner every so often and leave the children with a sitter, or they might invite their new friend to join the family for an excursion or outing, but at the end of each day, the parent returns to the children, alone. When kids have time alone with their biological parents, there is a sense of freedom from any masks or routines. They are not pressured to explain themselves or to put their guard up. They are home, and even though both biological parents are not physically present together anymore, the biological markers and patterns in a child's routine remain safe.

A wedding changes all of this. After the vows, dancing, and cake, the person who was formerly just a visitor now has a forever presence in the child's world, in the role of a parent. Suddenly, children find themselves sharing life with someone who brings new routines, new décor, and new patterns into their space. Recognizing the forever that will take place after their parent says "I do" may stir feelings of anxiety or sadness that can override some of the positive emotions previously communicated. Children may regress in their affection or attention toward you, either on the wedding day or shortly after. This behavior seems to contradict the linear timeline and process for strengthening a relational bond. It would seem logical that with a stronger commitment and more time together, greater closeness develops, but this logic does not always play out in a blended family process. This transition comes with its own unique dynamics.

Family transitions happen in a variety of ways. One of the biggest that families walk through is when parents prepare to bring a new baby into the world. If you have not personally been a family in this transition season, it is likely you have known one. I am right in the middle of this process with my own family. My husband and I are over the moon about the gift of a third child, and we anticipate with immense joy the jubilation that will follow this baby's arrival. We have two children who are also beaming with anticipatory exuberance. They ask hundreds of questions about how the baby is developing and what the baby will be like. They beg and plead to purchase baby clothes and gear months prior to the due date or baby shower festivities. Their friends all know about each kick they felt on Mommy's tummy. Even the grocery store clerks know they are going to be a big brother and big sister. Yes, there is excitement in something new, especially when it comes to adding family members to the mix. Yet, even in the excitement can lie unknowns, worries, and fears.

My son and I have our best conversations right after stories while snuggled close on his twin bed. In this season, he usually puts his hand on my belly and waits for a little kick. If it happens, his eyes widen with awe and his lips curve in a fascinated grin. We giggle and share our thoughts, eager to meet our little peanut.

"Are you so excited to be a big brother?" I asked him one night.

"I can't wait!" he replied.

"I know you are excited, but is there anything that makes you nervous about Mommy having a new baby?" I inquired.

"Kind of," he responded.

"What makes you nervous, honey?"

"I don't want you to love this baby more than you love me," he shared. I held him close and promised that my heart is not capable of running out of room, and that my feelings for him would never be compromised because of a new baby.

"You promise?" he asked.

"I promise!" I replied. This sweet conversation with my five-year-old son helped clarify what can be difficult to express in any season of change. New is exciting but can also come with elements of grief. Stepchildren often are excited about their parent's second chance for love. This excitement, however, is layered with worry, fear, and sometimes sadness. When the novelty wears off, reality sets in. A slew of emotional ups and downs follow as they process the permanence of the change.

My dad remarried during my senior year of high school. I remember scouring my closet for the right outfit. I must have tried on more than ten options as I searched for something that would make me feel put together. So many people I knew were coming; they would be watching me and, I feared, judging me as they observed my countenance. At eighteen, I was old enough to recognize I should be gracious and mature. After all, this day was not about me. I needed to stay positive.

Friends and family gathered to witness a bond of love and new beginning. I watched as the vows were said: "For better or worse, till death do us part." They were hard words for me to believe. How could they have meaning when the same promise was so recently broken between my parents after eighteen years of what I had seen as a happy marriage?

Choking back tears, I fought to present a façade of grace and acceptance. But behind my forced smile, I was experiencing painful heartache. While this day marked a new beginning for my dad, it felt like an ending for me. This was the end of feeling safe to be myself without the pressure of performing for someone new. It marked the end of my previous life as a nuclear family of six. I was about to leave for college, and when I returned, it would be to a foreign home, with a brand-new set of people and patterns I would have to learn. The changing patterns were not seasonal anymore; the wedding solidified the change as a permanent one and marked a new path that would forever change the direction of my life. I was apprehensive about what this direction would mean for my heart and my future. My new normal was unfolding. I understood that my dad and step-mom were happy together, but it was very challenging during this self-focused season of my adolescence to surrender my own vision of happiness to celebrate theirs. My heart was split. I was not ready to fully accept the reality of the changes unfolding.

A few years later, my mom prepared to walk down the aisle. This was no less difficult for my heart. Her wedding day carried a celebratory atmosphere. I enjoyed the reception and took advantage of the lively music on the dance floor. My posture was not pouty, but rather polite. I even invited a friend to join me for the festivities.

When comparing the two events, it may have appeared that my attitude was sullen and sad at my dad's wedding, yet celebratory and joyful at my mom's. This was not the reality. Neither wedding scene was devoid of grief. My feelings simply manifested on different timelines. With my dad's remarriage, my grief manifested *during* the wedding, but with my mom's, my grief manifested *after* the wedding.

My dad remarried before my mom did, and during this season, when I was at her house, I felt that I still had one safe haven that seemed normal. Before my mom remarried, I still could cling to an original piece of "us"—an "us" that reminded me of life before divorce. Before my mom's wedding, we could openly reminisce about the past without worrying about how it might affect someone else's feelings. We talked about our family—our original family—without including someone new. After my mom's wedding, this safe space changed. My stepdad moved in, and the just-us setting I had clung to was forever altered. This was when my grief manifested toward my mom.

Even though my countenance during each wedding day might have indicated that I was discontented with my dad's remarriage and that I favored my mom's, the reality of the situation was that I treated both of my parents and stepparents to less than kind behaviors and approached each from a somewhat selfish position. I was still in my grieving process when their second marriages took place. I had not yet moved into the acceptance stage, and thus exhibited behaviors that were less than appealing to both sides.

When children are not adapting to something new, they still have the freedom to cling to the old. After another marriage, the old is something that is lost, permanently. When parents remain single, children can still identify with the original pieces of their former life that help these fragments feel somewhat whole. When a new marriage takes place, the original pieces of life before divorce quickly disappear. A brand-new stage is set, while the heart of the child is often longing for the original script.

A Divided Heart

In most churches, an aisle literally divides the center of the sanctuary into two sides. This aisle is a very symbolic part of a wedding ceremony, so much so that the phrase "walk down the aisle" means to get married.

At the very beginning of a wedding, the bride and groom are in separate sections of the church. The groom enters the sanctuary with his groomsmen and the pastor, and they stand at the altar at one end of the aisle, eagerly awaiting the bride's entrance. The bride waits, traditionally with her father, at the opposite end of the aisle. As the wedding march begins to play, the bride and her father walk toward the groom with the bride's side of the family watching from one side and the groom's side on the other. At this point in the ceremony, there is division: An aisle splits two sides of the family-to-be and two individual people who are not yet united as one.

As the bride gets closer to her groom, anticipation builds, and when the father transfers his daughter's hand from his grip into the hand of her future husband, the couple reach the end of the division. An aisle no longer separates them. Promises are spoken as vows are exchanged, and the couple is dismissed and introduced as husband and wife, one flesh bound in marriage, in the presence of God and witnesses. Hands still clasped, they raise their arms in celebration and walk back down the aisle as a team. Families are united; two have become one. The guests leave the church together, no longer separated on two sides. It is a beautiful picture of God's

heart for a family and for a community bound by commitment and love.

When watching this tradition unfold in the context of a
second marriage, children sometimes struggle to embrace
the unity piece. Wedding symbolism speaks of togetherness,
yet a child's heart still feels divided. Remember the tension
I described feeling as I sat in the stands at my high school's
football championship game? This same emotional tug-of-
war exists for children when watching a parent's wedding
unfold.

Anatomically, the human heart is divided into four cham-
bers: two superior atria, which are low-pressure areas, and two
inferior ventricles that produce high pressures. This describes
the physical division of a human heart. The opposing high- and
low-pressure areas work together, allowing the heart to function as designed. When opposing pressures exist anatomically,
a heart works its best. Without both high- and low-pressure
functions, people are at risk of heart failure, so physically, the
presence of pressure is a healthy sign.

Emotionally, however, the pressure of a divided heart is
not healthy. Adjusting to a parent's new marriage may trigger
responses that lead to a child's heart becoming conflicted.
This internal conflict disrupts a child's feeling of peace. Mood
swings, rude behavior, rebellion, and anger can be a result of
this emotional conflict. One part of the child's heart believes
his or her parents deserve a second chance at lifelong love, but
the other part is deeply rooted in loyalty toward the parent's
first spouse. I remember feeling as though I was the reason for
the disrupting of peace in our family after each remarriage.
It was my internal peace that felt disrupted, and this struggle
manifested with external attitudes that were rarely positive. If
you are a stepparent who has experienced (or is experiencing)

a similar disruption of the peace, consider this internal conflict as a reason for it. This perspective may help you better understand why things may have changed after the wedding.

Another cause of emotional stress that children experience after a parent's new marriage is the pressure they sometimes feel to choose sides. Parents and stepparents sometimes compare a child's attitude toward their marriage to that of their former spouse. If this comparison reveals that one side is favored, confusion and pain usually follow.

Perceived Favorites

From my description of my differing conduct during each of my parents' wedding ceremonies, it might appear that I was showing favoritism. Internally, however, my heart was struggling in both circumstances. The attitudes and behaviors children exhibit on the actual wedding day are not always a fair or complete picture of the struggle taking place within them. It is like peeking in on social media to determine an accurate picture of a family. I have known people who, in the midst of a cancer diagnosis, or after learning about a partner's infidelity, appear not only content but extremely happy through an online lens. Pain is masked by pictures of vacation adventures or a child's big accomplishment. Smiles persist through incredibly heavy heartache. Yet, without both the complete picture and accurate data about the circumstances, assumptions become someone's reality. Often this one-sided lens is the only access a couple has to their children and stepchildren when they spend time with the other parent and stepparent. This can lead to the perception of favoritism, which comes with the risk of feeling jealous or confused about why the other parent combo is getting the best of the kids.

A friend of ours recently walked through a divorce with her three children. She remarried before her husband did and took to social media to showcase how happy the girls were with their new stepdad. Pictures from a recent tropical vacation populated her social media pages, and each one featured beaming smiles. We are also friends of her former husband, who at the time was not yet remarried. He often shared his discouragement regarding the kids' attitudes when they were with him. After all, he was their biological dad, but he began to feel less connected to them than a brand-new stepparent. The smiles he saw in the pictures weren't always displayed during their time with him. He was frustrated. Even though he was extremely intentional in creating meaningful moments with his girls, they always seemed to have better things to say about the other couple.

If your experience feels anything like this one, try not to let it defeat you. Remember that you only get a small glimpse of the children when they are with the other family. Most likely, the other parent and stepparent are receiving an equal number of challenges but simply are not posting them for the world to see.

Another inquiry about this topic came to me via email from a couple who were very affected by this perceived favoritism in their home. After teaching a blended family workshop, I received this question:

Dear Lauren,

Why do the kids (both our biological and stepchildren) seem so compassionate and loving to the other parent and not toward us? They seem to be picking favorites. The most difficult part is that they are favoring our ex-spouses, who were the ones who left both of us for another person.

I imagine there is an incredible amount of hurt and frustration felt by both stepparents and parents when they are treated with disdain and disrespect—especially if this behavior is commonplace for one couple while the other side appears to be welcomed with open arms. Here are a few considerations to think about if this is a struggle you face.

First, it is likely that the favoritism you feel is happening is perceived but not quite accurate. When every outing with the other side appears to be fun and easy, remember that your lens is capturing only a small segment of that child's experience. Children are not as open about sharing their struggles as they are about sharing their joys. This is why at the dinner table it is much easier to get the daily highlights out of your children than it is to get them to share about their day's frustrations.

Second, it is more natural for children to favor the parent and stepparent combo with whom they have less routine day-to-day interaction. Logically, this does not make sense. It seems more likely that children would form a closer bond with, and express more love toward, the people they see most regularly and who are present in their everyday lives. So why do parent and stepparent combos get the best of the children whom they see the least? Sometimes, this type of favoritism happens because when time is limited with one side of the family, it is more likely that time is spent nurturing adventure and outings rather than nurturing routines and responsibilities. It is easy and natural for a child to favor parents who are not disciplining them or who are not outlining expectations. Children rarely express their gratitude for parents who set boundaries and hold children accountable to high standards. I have never been thanked by my children for following through with a punishment.

Perceived favoritism can certainly feel hurtful and frustrating as you work to cultivate a loving blended family culture.

Be cautious, however, when trying to understand or justify this perception as a whole. The word *favorite* indicates that a *better than* or *worse than* culture exists. If I ask my children what their favorite dessert is, I am forcing them to rank one option over another. This question in itself is part of the tension children experience with blended family dynamics. The presence, or appearance, of favoritism communicates that children feel the need to pick a side. Feeling less-than is not a fun experience for anyone, especially when the side perceived to be winning does not appear to deserve it.

Consider how this mindset creates an unfair environment for your children and stepchildren. They are the ones who must juggle both sides and give each a fair shot to have equal access to their heart. It is never easy to feel like the ones who are routinely experiencing only the difficult parts of a child's behavior. Even so, try not to force them to explain or defend themselves. You do not want to put children in the center of the fight and heighten the pressure they feel when they truly are trying to root for both sides. Children do believe their parents deserve to be happy in another marriage. Sometimes, however, when parents commit to their new happily-ever-after, children feel like they have to give up their own.

--------------------- CHAPTER 3 ---------------------
TAKEAWAY SUMMARY

1. Remember that children often feel divided in the face of a parent's new marriage. Part of their heart truly desires that their mom or dad gets a second chance at lasting love, yet part of it struggles with the reality of the change.

2. A wedding solidifies the permanence of divorce and forever shuts the door on the hope a child may be clinging to for reconciliation. Recognize that some of the struggle is not about the marriage, but rather the finality of their new family dynamics.

3. It is natural to feel confusion or jealousy when children appear to be favoring one parent's new marriage over the other's. Be cautious when trying to uncover or explain why, and try to remember that doing so puts the kids in a difficult position of ranking one experience over another.

4

It's Not About You

> There were intruders in my family tree, and I was not able to grieve the loss of my original branches without a new audience. My stepmom's character was acceptable to me; however, the role she now played was not.

Nothing shows character like the sidelines of youth sports. The pregame posture is one of anticipation as parents cue their phones to capture the glorious moment that everyone on social media will applaud. If you are anything like me, you try hard to temper your emotions so you don't develop a negative reputation. You know the kind of sideline parent I'm describing: the type who yells at the teenage referee, who is volunteering his time to build his résumé for college. These parents are known for screaming at and to their kids, as if hearing their parent's voice will prompt the game-winning score. Such parents try not to care, yet they care so much that even a loss in the recreational sports of seven-year-olds throws them into a passive-aggressive angry cyclone. Many of us have secretly judged those parents. Truth be told, I have been one of these parents. For those of you who identify with this deeply rooted competitive spirit, even when the stakes are low, emotions run hot. Each season I gravitate toward the parents who share a fierce fire for the win. During a recent soccer season, I spoke with one such mom who would soon connect with my heart in a different capacity.

We unpacked our canvas chairs and layered ourselves in blankets. The wind chill was brutal, and we snuggled together to stay warm. Our stainless-steel coffee cups steamed in our palms. During the team warm-up, we settled into our sideline seats and exchanged a familiar greeting. "Good morning. It looks like it's going to be a chilly one," I said. "We're excited to have you guys back this week. We truly missed having one of our star players while you guys were out. How are you?"

"It was a little stressful this morning," she answered. "Amy's mom is coming to watch today; I can tell Amy is nervous. She asked Coach if she could play goalie, because she doesn't want to mess up in front of her mom. We'll see. It will be a miracle if she even shows."

For two seasons I had interfaced with this family, and for the first time, I learned that this woman was a stepparent.

"Does Amy's mom make it to many of the games?" I asked.

"No, she's only seen her once in the last nine months."

Her tone indicated frustration. I could hear her defeat and sense her confusion. I could picture her determination to earn the affection and respect that she deserved yet was so far from experiencing. As the news of their family structure sunk in, I turned to her and said, "Please know, it's not about you. You are an incredible and necessary part of her life." I knew in that moment that we had started a conversation in which I could encourage from the perspective of a child.

Know that no matter how abundant your love, how consistent your presence, or how strategic your discipline, the process of earning a stepchild's affection often proves challenging. Hold your head high, and receive these words: It is not about you.

Amy's story is not an isolated one. Recently, I was in a conference setting when a gentleman shared his experience with me. He told part of his story, explaining how he had fought to make his marriage work but went through a divorce after his previous spouse left him for someone else. The heartache and defeat were palpable. He inquired to gain insight about why his children were so kind to the parent who left, while he and his current wife got the brunt of their anger and disrespect. How could the parents who were providing stability, financial security, a spiritual foundation, and consistent presence be the ones the kids regularly hurt? Why does the parent who is absent get to be the hero?

In response to both scenarios, I assured the stepparents with these words: "Try to remember it is not about you."

Trying to pinpoint what you are doing wrong is often wasted energy. Why? Because the pushback you feel is rarely personal. Whether you are treating kids to vacations, taking on all their chores as a secret pact, buying them the iPhone they have always wanted, or intentionally engaging with their friends to be liked, a stepchild's heart is not primarily wooed by your actions. Their struggle is not with you as a *person*, but rather with your *position*. It may give you more freedom in your process to know that the position you hold in a stepchild's life is one that no personality profile can change. You are the person they view as taking the place of their mom or dad. You hold a position that no longer leaves room for the hope of reconciliation to occur in their nuclear family. In talking with stepparents, I hear how frustrated they feel when the energy and intention they put into a pursuit for affection falls flat. They feel like they can never win. If this happens in your experience, know that you are seen. Know that you matter. Know that your labor is not in vain. Relational fruit may take a long time to manifest. In some cases, it may not look the way you envisioned it. Keeping to your position will help children trust that you are there for them and respectful of their timeline.

Stop Surrendering Power

I am an avid football fan and was raised with a Denver Broncos flag flying high on Sundays. On game days we huddled together on the couch, wearing John Elway number seven jerseys with a cooler full of Orange Crush soda nearby. Dad walked us through the roster and helped us match the players to their respective jersey numbers. I became a fan not only of the team, but also of the individual players. I felt like I knew them. We spun stories about how incredible it would be to meet them in person. Elway was one of the three famous people I would want to invite to my celebrity dinner party. Being a fan is fun.

In a healthy nuclear family setting, children watch their parents function as a team. Watching their patterns, and experiencing their coaching styles, creates a culture that is familiar and trustworthy. My dad's coaching style was different from my mom's, yet both regularly assured us that they were working together. When the divorce happened, the well-known coaching staff I was used to disassembled. Roles were undefined, practices were on different turf, and pregame routines disappeared. I remember trying to capture this experience with my counselor when I was sixteen.

She asked me, "What do you need from your parents right now to help you adjust to the divorce?" I think my answer surprised her.

I replied, "I need them to tell me to take out the trash." I answered this way because for fifteen years, Monday was trash day. I collected all the wastebaskets upstairs while my brothers tag-teamed the basement and my sister helped with the main floor. Our coaches told us what was expected, and our team always managed to get the trash out before the trucks came. Now, after both parents had moved, trash day was no longer on Mondays. I did not even know when the trash collector came at each house, and most likely, I was not home to help.

In this life stage I spent much more time with friends at their houses, because my home was unfamiliar turf, which I often avoided. I had always seen our family functioning as a winning team. After the divorce, this perspective changed. I was unfamiliar with our family's roster, was unsure about which coach's voice to follow, and when stepparents entered the scene, all I knew was surface data and statistics from the draft. It was a rebuilding season, and if you have ever watched a championship team during a rebuilding year, you desperately long for the days when you knew you could expect a win.

On December 3, 2017, CBS News reported the result of a rebuilding season for the Denver Broncos: A loss to the Miami Dolphins was their eighth in a row, and this type of losing streak had not happened to this team since 1967, when they lost nine straight games. After witnessing this game, and the seven before it, how could I endure the disappointment? It felt so surreal when just two years earlier we had celebrated with close to one million fans in a downtown Denver parade as Super Bowl 50 champions. I endured this long streak of losses by making a conscious choice, and a concerted effort, not to continue surrendering the power I previously had given to each game's result.

When the Broncos' score has power in my life, a loss ruins my entire day. I grunt and grumble around the house with a short fuse and sometimes end up doing the dishes with a bit more passion. Pots and pans bang together, and I quickly recognize that my actions disrupt the peace and create chaos. If I am in this state of mind and my kids ask me a question, I fly off the handle, as if they are the problem. Power is often something we assign to people. If we give power to a football team, that team's performance directly affects our mood. People sometimes give power to strangers serving them at a restaurant. If they fail to refill a drink efficiently, it ruins the entire dining experience. We give power to highway traffic. A car accident that slows your commute engenders anger, frustration, and sometimes even rage.

In stepfamilies, the negative beliefs, attitudes, and actions of stepchildren can have tremendous power over you. Rather than giving so much power to the children, work toward letting that go. The behaviors exhibited toward you, or sometimes even against you, are rarely fair and often are painful. Once you understand that as a stepparent your *position* affects the children more than your *personality* does, you can begin to release the pressure you might feel to actively win their favor. Don't surrender to the children the power over your emotions. Remembering this perspective will help you harness confidence in a position that often feels vulnerable and resented.

Growing up as one of four children, I had countless opportunities to tattle and try to get my siblings in trouble. Two of my brothers especially enjoyed the opportunity to push my buttons. Whether they were ruining my favorite doll's hairstyle or tormenting my hamster, Tippy, I would run to my mom. Rather than intervening with a punishment, she would tell me, "Stop giving them so much power." It was frustrating to know that even though their actions were hurting me, I was the one who was expected to adapt my behavior. But much to my surprise, doing so helped minimize the conflict. Refusing to acknowledge my brothers' attempts to get under my skin took all the fun out of it for them. Without my dramatic response, they stopped.

Little did I know, the very same words that frustrated me as a child empowered me as an adult. I know there are behaviors in your stepchildren you would like to change. Kids act ungrateful, say things about you that are hurtful, ignore you in front of their peers, or disregard you completely. How paralyzing this must feel after countless efforts to connect. Rather than feeling like you want *their* behavior to change, try the method my mom used when we wanted our siblings' behavior to stop. Take back your power; try not to let the emotional processes of a child affect your own confidence or value.

Don't Try to Change Who You Are

There are many negative brands and associations connected with the stepparent role. Disney, for example, routinely typecasts stepparents as evil, ugly, and villainous. From Cinderella's evil stepmother to Snow White's wicked queen, this role rarely receives positive press. Know, however, that in a child's mind you are not viewed as evil. Instead, you are viewed as new. Children respond differently to new situations. My kids remind me of this regularly.

My daughter, Lia, has been watchful and observant since she was born. Even before she could talk, she used to stare people down with her enormous blue eyes and furrow her brow, as if communicating she was not so sure of you. Before trying anything new, she asks direct and detailed questions. Even after her questions are answered, she proceeds with caution. She embraces new opportunities confidently but requires time and preparation before committing. When Lia was three, we clearly saw these characteristics in action as we approached a highly anticipated ski school adventure. For months she waited in great expectation of a promised full-day lesson. When the day finally arrived, she was hesitant. Even with all the excitement, Lia was tentative. At the check-in desk she asked us to remind her about the weather, double-check her clothing, assess her instructor, and inquire about snacks. Eventually, when she had the information she needed, Lia embraced an epic ski day.

My son, Jace, has a very different way of processing new things. He trusts immediately, loves spontaneity, and goes with the flow. I remember being at a water park in Florida right before his fourth birthday. He saw some older children trying a zip line from a platform high above the water. Without reservation, he marched to reserve his spot in line, grabbed the handle, and confidently jumped off the platform. He soared through the air, squealing with glee. The force of the handle hitting its end point launched him high above the water into a backflip. When he surfaced, I was certain he would burst into tears. Instead, to my surprise, he popped out of the water and exclaimed, "That was awesome! Can I do it again?"

Your stepparent role is new, and although it is much more complex than a day in ski school or a water park ride, children will process this new role differently. Some may furrow their brow, roll their eyes, and clearly communicate that they do not trust you. Others may quickly melt your heart with compliments and affection in a very short time frame. However you are received, recognize that children are engaging their own personal process. They are not always responding to yours.

What do I mean by your process? Stepparents might feel like it is their responsibility to connect with their stepchildren through an incremental checklist: If they learn what the child enjoys, engage the child in said activity, and bond with the child through this activity, then they will gain the child's trust and affection. Sometimes your envisioned process fails to produce the desired results. What can you do in situations like this to experience a better result?

Once you understand that as a stepparent your position affects the children more than your personality, you can begin to release the pressure you might feel to use actions to win their favor. Additionally, observe and recognize the patterns you see in each of your stepchildren's processes. Watch how they approach unfamiliar situations, and take note of patterns that bolster confidence and success. Look for unique indicators in your relationship with each child, and when you find one that brings you hope, try to replicate it. Your stepchildren may respond to you differently. Become a student of what works best for each. Often you hear that time will heal. Although time is part of the healing process, remember that it is how you invest that time that changes things.

Keep to Your Post

I love to work out and am known to push myself physically and fight through pain. This wiring drew me into a local CrossFit community shortly after my son was born. I quickly became an enthusiast. The encouragement and passion in the gym were electric, and anytime I saw a movement I thought I could never master, a patient coach walked me through the mechanics and equipped me for success. CrossFit is fast, intense, and group focused. For me, these qualities made it a great workout option. Yoga, conversely, requires steadfast focus, patient endurance, and individual discipline. I have attempted yoga before but have never been able to stick with it. For me, staying still feels like wasted energy. However, a skilled yoga athlete knows that staying still and holding your position is the very discipline that builds strength and produces results.

Sometimes a stepparent's greatest strength comes from remaining steadfast and still in their position. This often produces the best relational results. Rather than desperately striving to adapt your personality to fit what you think the children want, stay in a position that honors who you are. I have never been a stepparent myself, but I am a stepchild. I understand what kinds of conflict arise from striving to impress. You spend a lot of time spinning your wheels, only to find that regardless of what you try, you still feel rejected and hurt.

Do not lose heart. Understanding the importance of position, not personality, is more productive in your progress toward a healthy relationship.

My stepmom is, and always has been, kind, gracious, generous, and supportive, yet for many years, my responses to her rarely mirrored these virtues. When I was in college, I learned she was expecting a baby boy. She shared the news over the phone and communicated how excited and thankful she was to have me as this baby's sister. Not wanting to exclude me from her joy, she sent updates and exchanged phone calls. I remember receiving the birth announcement in my college PO box. I looked at the picture of this beautiful baby boy, yet I struggled to know how to respond. I do not remember feeling angry, sad, or bitter about this announcement—in fact, I did not really feel anything. I was moving along in my rapid college rhythm, focused on my dreams and goals, not paying much attention to the needs of my stepmom. I may have called her but failed to send a gift or greet this baby with much pomp and circumstance.

To this day, I recognize that my lack of acknowledgment and celebration is one of the greatest hurts I caused my stepmom, though none of my actions were an intentional attack on her character.

As an adult, I am better equipped to communicate that my motives for treating her negatively had nothing to do with her, but rather, everything to do with me. I was in Texas starting my second year of college; she was in Colorado living in a different city from the one where I grew up. I was focused on friendships and school; she was focused on the incredible miracle of childbirth. I was trying to determine my current and future identity, yet the identity of my family was becoming an enigma. When I visited home, I felt like a stranger, walking on eggshells to make sure everyone stayed happy.

I felt it incredibly unfair that a decision my parents had made without us children would forever interrupt the direction I dreamed my family could go. There were intruders in my family tree, and I was not able to grieve the loss of my original branches without a new audience. My stepmom's character was acceptable to me; however, the role she now played was not. It was her position that threatened acceptance, not the person she was. She tried to move toward me and include me in one of her life's greatest joys; I was simply not ready to respond.

Adopting an intentional and progressive role seems like the most logical way to earn affection. When pursuing someone romantically, you enter his or her world, become a student of his or her passions, and move toward one another. Coming from my experience as a stepchild, I might argue the opposite approach. As you pursue the affection of a child who is not eager to receive you, your steps toward them may inadvertently cause them to step away.

The stepparent/stepchild dynamics are very different from that of a nuclear family. Consent in a stepparent/stepchild relationship may sometimes feel one-sided. The parent desires so much to be welcomed and loved, and genuinely cares for the children—who sometimes do not reciprocate as graciously. I do not suggest moving away from the children in your blended family, nor am I implying that it is wrong to express affection and to understand their needs. Rather, I am suggesting you use your position as an advocate and not as an inhibitor. What I mean by that is keep to your post. Stand confident and present, but do not move from your post until invited by the child. It is much like the analogy of staying in your position on a sports team.

Growing up, I played competitive soccer. My coach mostly placed me as a center midfielder. This was an offensive position in which scoring was possible and often made me the star. I loved the attention and the spotlight that playing this position allowed. But as my team developed and changed, my coach saw a need for me to move to the position of right wing. I was truly disappointed in this switch. Now I would have to pass the ball—most often to the center midfielder. In doing so, I watched another person hit the net and steal my glory. In the beginning, I always wanted to leave my position as wing and run to center field, carrying the ball to the net with my own skill rather than showcasing another's.

"Lauren, stay in your position," my coach would yell from the sidelines. "Be patient; get to the sideline." Grudgingly, I would adapt and listen to his instructions, but I felt my new role was not showcasing my talents or allowing me to help the team in any way. As I learned to hold my position, wait for the pass, and move the ball up the field, I recognized that my speed and agility were assisting my team to double its scoring stats. I learned to love my new role, but I had to be patient in waiting for the ball to come to me to make my move. It turns out I was more effective as a right wing than I ever was as a center midfielder. Our team did very well that season.

In the same way, hold your position as a stepparent. When the children toss the ball in your direction, make your move. More often than not, patience and diligence in this role will enable you to score many more wins with him or her and feel like your family's MVP rather than the ball hog. As you stay steadfast and present, your stepchild is likely to move in your direction. You cannot refuse forever someone who loves you well. Remember that not all children will keep the ball from you. Some might pass it right away and even celebrate when you score. Whichever situation you find yourself in, remember that the rebuilding stage of any team requires intention, endurance, persistence, and time.

Position Your Marriage Well

One of the most important positions you hold as a stepparent does not involve your stepchildren, but rather, your partner. This is your position as a husband or a wife. The reason you are a stepparent is because you married a child's mom or dad. It is normal to assume that because a previous marriage ended, the children did not see a model of love and partnership reflected the first time around. This may or may not be true. Either way, your position in a new marriage allows a platform for you and your spouse to model a thriving relationship. It is vital for children to witness a healthy marriage relationship, and hopefully, with a fresh start, you and your spouse are positioned well to demonstrate some of the healthier patterns that may or may not have existed before. Even so, please recognize that it is not your role to convince your stepchildren that you are the answer to all the brokenness in the first marriage. If you approach your position this way, you risk triggering resentment in your stepchildren. Here is why this happens.

First of all, the messenger matters. When a stepparent takes the role of a marriage mentor, children may resist your advice. Portraying your marriage as better than that of their biological parents', or pointing out that their biological parent is so much happier with you, can make children feel disrespected or even hurt. Even if your claims are valid, communicating these messages invalidates the child's previous family makeup. Even some of the most toxic relationships have good moments. Kids fully understand that their parents did not do marriage perfectly. Many likely were exposed to very destructive and harmful behaviors that their parents exhibited toward one another. Regardless of the negative realities, children have the right to hold on to the good.

The word *better* signifies a comparison; if they continually hear "better" from you, there is a risk that they label their former family structure as *worse*. It is appropriate to model behaviors that are better than they may have been in a previous marriage, but be sensitive when verbalizing this sentiment in a teaching or training role. I imagine that stepparents feel responsible to help kids recognize the differences between a healthy and unhealthy marriage. After all, your assumption may be that you are one of the only healthy marriage models this child will ever see. I cannot speak for all children, but after my parents' divorce, I witnessed many healthy marriage models. A community of friends loved me extravagantly during this transitional time. I was invited into their lives and saw many marriages that were working well. You absolutely are one of the marriage models that children are observing, but it is likely that you are not the only one.

The second reason taking the role of a marriage mentor for your stepchildren may not produce the intended result is that doing so might confuse the role of savior. This posturing puts an enormous amount of pressure on you to be the catalyst for establishing their future marriage legacy. There is no doubt that witnessing a model of a healthy marriage may be part of their redemptive story, but it does not have to be the whole of it. The weight of this responsibility is an extremely heavy burden to put on your shoulders. Rather than instructing them about *how* to make marriage work, prioritize conversation around *who* designed marriage to work. Ultimately, understanding God's voice gives children the power and perspective they will need to establish a solid marriage legacy in their future. God cares more about our children and stepchildren than we do, and He can be trusted with their lives.

Most of the stepparents I know genuinely want what is best for their stepchildren. They endure a lot of hurt as they delicately navigate their position. Cyclical hurt becomes exhausting and feels defeating, often adding stress to your marriage. It is vital that you nurture your marriage relationship with utmost care and try not to let the relational discord between you and your stepchildren interfere with your second chance at a healthy and thriving relationship with your spouse. Protect time to connect. Set boundaries and agreements that allow you to engage with one another in ways that do not involve talking about or being present with kids.

My parents both have expressed some of the guilt they carried, knowing that their decision to divorce directly impacted us as children—even into adulthood. Carrying this guilt might create a subconscious or conscious favoritism or prioritization of your children over your spouse. This balance is certainly difficult to navigate; however, a second divorce amplifies the pain and has the risk of negating all the energy and effort you put into the blended family process. Eventually your children will not live at home and will create their own adult life path, so do your best to prioritize your marriage and not allow a child's behavior to tear you apart.

--------------------------- CHAPTER 4 ---------------------------
TAKEAWAY SUMMARY

1. The hurtful things stepchildren say are not justified or fair, but do your best to surrender the amount of power you allow stepchildren to have regarding your value and identity.

2. Embrace who you are without striving to adapt your personality to please your stepchildren.

3. Hold your position patiently, and be postured to receive affirmation and affection from stepchildren when they are ready to offer it.

4. Release some of the pressure you feel to model the perfect marriage for your stepchildren. Nurture your marriage as a high priority, and work to approach the marriage role separately from your parenting role.

5

Identity Crisis

My family identity was torn, and the characteristics of my pre-divorce world no longer fit into either family picture.

When you type *personality test* into an internet search, you discover a wealth of quizzes populated with questions that reveal clues about your most authentic self. To achieve an accurate assessment, truthful answers are required. This test is easy. You breeze through the questions without reservation because there are no wrong answers. Complete freedom to choose characteristics is yours. If you are anything like me, there is excitement about viewing your results. The program tallies a summary that validates your makeup and makes you feel extraordinary. It is always entertaining for me to watch others read their personality profile summaries. They nod, whisper "yes," and murmur phrases like, "That is so true!" I believe that everyone desires to be fully known and authentically understood. Sometimes a printed personality profile summary enables people to see, in writing, the traits that help secure their identity. Your sense of identity, however, develops long before you ever take an assessment. It begins even before you take your first breath.

Ask any parent to recall the experience of meeting their child for the first time. Watch the expression in their eyes and you will see the clarity and power in reminiscing about that moment. Rarely does a parent respond by saying, "I don't really know what that moment was like." Instead, you see eyes light up, bodies lean in, and hearts swell. An invitation to announce your child's life story is one of the very best. Josh and I had our first encounter with the magic of this moment in the spring of 2010. The anticipation was palpable as I paced up and down our neighborhood sidewalks trying to discern "go time" signs. Pacing led nowhere, and patience was wearing thin, so as a distraction we accepted an invitation from friends to join them for a night of bowling. At forty weeks' pregnant, throwing a fifteen-pound ball down an alley was not advised by our doctor. Taking precautions, I sat out and passed on the opportunity to play. I was content being a spectator and cheering from the plastic vinyl bar stool while drinking a soda. It was a good distraction while waiting for labor to begin. Sitting still did not come easily for me, so when a friend offered *just one* of her frames for me to participate, I caved. One frame never hurt anyone, so I accepted the invitation.

I stood up, approached the lane, and positioned myself behind the painted boundary line. With my best pre-labor form, I released the iridescent pink ball and sent it flying straight down the center of the alley. Eight pins fell to the ground, and I threw my hands in the air to celebrate. At that very moment, with my hands in the air, my water broke. Surprised, wide-eyed, and in disbelief, I thanked our friends for the invite, grabbed Josh's hand, and waddled swiftly toward the parking lot. We were about to have a baby. This was the very moment we had dreamt about, and it was happening right now.

The following day, our lives forever changed. The doctor placed our newborn in Josh's hands. "We have a baby girl!" he exclaimed. Right after he revealed her gender, he assured me, "Don't worry, we can have another one that looks like you." Our daughter—the spitting image of her father—was beautiful, and she was family. Knit together perfectly, with intentionality. That was our moment. The moment we met Lia Emily Reitsema, born May 8, weighing 6 pounds 12 ounces, at 4:07 p.m. This began our daughter's process of learning and knowing her identity. She is a Reitsema. She has Dutch, German, and Italian roots. Her parents will teach her to ski. She will root for the Texas Christian University Horned Frogs. She will sleep under the stars for a minimum of five nights every summer. Our family will protect her and create a safe environment for her to thrive. She will participate in further defining our family, and we will provide structure and cues for her to define her own someday.

Most children begin their life the same way. They are born or adopted into a family. Their identity immediately starts to develop as they take on a name and occupy a space created for them as a son or daughter. Children do not have the power to change this identity-shaping experience. People can adapt their environment or expose themselves to new environments, but they will always be who they are. A large part of who they are stems from family. After a divorce, your family identity is fractured. It is difficult to define where you fit.

Disrupted Roles

Imagine the following scenario from a vocational standpoint. You are a faithful employee and have worked in your position for twelve years. You started as an intern and looked to your manager for assignments, progress measurements, and growth opportunities. During your role as an intern, the task lists that appeared in your email rarely bothered you. In fact, the guidelines helped you focus and apply your skills to measurable and attainable goals that helped in assessing your performance. Your work ethic and consistency gelled your team as a unit. Each year brought new opportunities, some including celebrated promotions. Earning more responsibility, you were entrusted with authority regarding team decisions, and people pursued you for creative problem-solving ideas and a final say in decisions about the company brand.

At the beginning of the new year, you are thriving as an empowering leader. People know you, not only at the office but in the community your business serves. You are about to begin your thirteenth consecutive year with the company when, without your input, your manager is fired. Corporate brings in someone new. After taking the time to move into his new office, your new boss emails you with a list of menial tasks, restructures the company mission statement, and threatens the very existence of your job. He barely knows your skill set, yet he is put in charge of setting your quarterly expectations and monitoring your progress. Although he has not played a role in your employee development, he enjoys bragging about you and taking some of the credit for your work. You have lost your voice. You miss your old team, and your fire feels extinguished. How would you feel as this employee? What kinds of labels might you put on your new manager? How would you navigate the changes?

Now consider this scenario playing out in a family instead of in a vocational setting. Instead of twelve years as an employee, imagine a twelve-year-old son. This young man is accustomed to a predetermined set of expectations and is aware of the disciplinary repercussions when he breaks protocol. Approaching adolescence, he worked with his parents to help define the tricky balance of growing independence. New freedoms came with greater responsibility. He received the cell phone he desperately wanted for his birthday, but only after discussing and signing the contract his parents drafted for setting appropriate boundaries.

Meeting expectations meant more independence, and in middle school, independence was an exciting privilege. Instead of always telling him things, his parents began asking him things. His opinion mattered. He had a say in answering questions such as, "Where do you think we should go to celebrate Grandma's birthday?" "What would you like for dinner this week?" "Where would you like to go this year for our family vacation?" Not only had he worked for years to develop his voice, but he finally understood how to assert it in a way that is respectful and respected. He has discovered his voice, and his parents are listening to it. He has a strong familial role. He is known; he is loved.

Halfway through the school year, his parents tell him they are separating. He feels like he has been hit by a Mack truck, and after a very short transition time, new "managers" enter the picture and begin to dictate the very culture of his family. To complicate matters, he is regularly labeled as selfish and hard to manage, even though his role had nothing to do with the restructuring. His voice is not only gone, but it has been taken from him without permission.

When adapting to a stepparent's role, children may feel like they are amidst a major company overhaul. Sometimes they feel like they have no say in the hiring process. Even when they are invited into the interview before commitment, they quickly realize they do not have authority in the final decision. The brand is unfamiliar, the location is often new, and the corporate culture is confusing. They have committed their hands to the work of a family unit and are taking the steps necessary to accept that this change is forever. It is not surprising that this situation is a difficult one. However, there are strategies you can employ to make the transition better. In his book *The 7 Habits of Highly Effective People*, Stephen Covey writes, "Seek first to understand, then to be understood."[1] Use your own voice to empower and not to enrage. The following suggestions may be helpful ways to affirm and continue to rebuild your stepchild's fragmented family identity.

Identify the Fragments

I was sixteen when my parents finalized their divorce. For sixteen years, I was a part of the Klein family. I knew what it meant to be a Klein. Work hard, celebrate victories, strive to win, and always use manners. Sundays were for church and family meetings. Dad's radio was set to country music on 850 KOA; Mom's typically played pop Christian hits or broadcasted talk-radio personalities debating the latest political trends. If we wanted to know what was for dinner, we checked the calendar behind a magnet on the fridge. Weeknight meals were determined on the first of each month. Each child chose his or her preferred dish in a rotating fashion around the kitchen table. Mom would write the menu selection on each calendar square and move through the week until an entire month was full. Dinners were done—no mystery, no arguing. Grades mattered, and we worked hard to perform our best in school. On birthdays, the guest of honor chose the menu and sat in the chair with a balloon tied to its frame. The "You are Special" blue-and-red-trimmed china plate marked your birthday place setting. For my sixteen years, we nurtured our identity as a family, which brought safety, security, and clarity. Countless others also knew the Klein family. They knew what we looked like and what we valued; they knew our behaviors and our roles.

I loved being a Klein. It came with a sense of pride and accomplishment. I never felt invisible. I never felt alone. I rarely ever was alone. With three siblings and parents involved in the community, there was always someone around. People saw you coming and going. People introduced themselves in the grocery store, and they checked in when something was hard. It felt great to be known.

Divorce did not change my last name, but it did change everything about our family identity. Almost overnight, we were divided. Our parents' social circles now rotated around one single person, not a married couple. These expanding communities did not know, and never would know, the other parent. We were the kids who were around sometimes and disappeared at others. We spoke of divorce, brokenness, and sadness. We were no longer known as the productive and accomplished children of a fabulous family. Instead, we were the kids people felt sorry for, whose story became hard. The most difficult part was that we had no power to change it.

For a season, I held on to the Klein identity with confidence. I was preparing to leave for college, and it was my chance for a fresh start, a chance to be known outside of the pitied *life is so hard* attitude of people we had always known. Being a Klein could be new again, and college roommates would never see the divide of a before and an after. Launching into this season gave hope to rebuild and reclaim parts of my original family identity. Visits home, however, disrupted this new normal. Remarriage directed each of my biological parents to create a new family identity, but for us, as the kids before divorce, our identity became further confused.

My sophomore year of college, my mom married a Scotsman. His passion for his roots manifested in every part of his life. A plaid table runner was now a central decoration in our dining room, and a small Scottish terrier roamed throughout the house. Hunter-green and navy tartan-patterned pillows replaced the old floral ones that used to be on the couch. Scottish history books rested in the center of the coffee table. For him, this décor carried rich symbolism and meaning. I did not share such sentiment. We were not Scottish! Bagpipes made me think of funerals, and plaid of private school uniforms. Yet now these cultural identifiers marked Mom as a MacAllan and seemingly dwarfed our Italian roots.

Also, while I was away in college, my dad and stepmom began their own family, welcoming a baby boy. When he became old enough, they recorded his voice on the home answering machine. I remember calling one time and hearing a childlike falsetto tone recite the words, "Hi, you've reached the Klein family. We're not home, so please leave a message and we will get back to you as soon as we can." It struck me that the "we" did not include me. It would never include me. I would never be the person returning one of those home phone calls. The Klein family was now a four-year-old little boy, his mom, and his father—his father, who just happened to have four older kids from a previous life and a previous marriage. Yes, our last name was the same, but our family dynamics and experiences were vastly different. I felt like I did not fit in either family setting. On one side of my family I was known as a "first-marriage kid" who was around only on holidays. On the other side I was an extension of a Scottish clan, absorbing traditions and markings of a country I had only known because of its association with famous golf courses. My family identity was torn, and the characteristics of my pre-divorce world no longer fit into either family picture. *Where do I fit? Which family do I belong to?* My parents had a chance to start over and begin to define new roles and new names. As a child, my only option was to stay in limbo.

Study Past Family History

Anyone who knows someone under the age of ten is most likely familiar with the song "Let It Go," made famous by the popular Disney ice princess Elsa. The catchy chorus is intended to mark a new season, one empowered by future potential, not one inhibited by past pain. I believe this posturing is a helpful one in the healing process for adults after remarrying. Thinking about past spouses and past traditions may break boundaries and is not a healthy strategy for moving forward in your marriage. In the stepparent role, however, studying the past experiences of the children is a vital component of cultivating a healthy connection. Here is why: For children of divorce, the past does not stay in the past. Their past family history is still part of their present reality. In fact, these identity-affirming routines most likely will also be a part of their future.

What do I mean by identity-affirming routines? Remember the story I shared with my counselor about wishing my parents would ask me to take out the trash? The reason I answered her question with that response had nothing to do with my wanting to do more chores. Rather, the trash-day routine validated my identity as a critical teammate in a necessary task. There was no plan B in our routine to accomplish this chore, and I felt needed and known when called upon to participate. In my post-divorce world, I was no longer needed in the trash-day routine. Someone else could easily accomplish this task; I no longer fit in a previously valued role. When your stepchildren share about their pre-divorce family experiences, they are not simply sharing routines and roles—they are sharing pieces of their identity.

Some of the best leadership advice I have ever received is that people own what they help to create. Pre-divorce, children are participants in their family routines. They are part owners in a family brand, and this brand has helped form and shape their identity. Initially, when stepparents take over in a new parental role, the children do not have ownership in the routines; rather, they function as bystanders. Help move stepchildren from spectators to participants by allowing children to speak about their past family brand and discuss how they contributed to its success. This information can help you identify identity-affirming roles you can incorporate into your blended family structure.

Think about your own experience with your family when you were growing up. What stories do your parents tell about the day they first met you? What were the rules and expectations in your household? What cues did you follow to shape the person you became as an adult? Whatever the family structure, most people can recall which position they played and its corresponding roles and responsibilities. These expectations help affirm that value, and shape who you become.

Think about how you would answer the following questions pertaining to your own family's experience; then repeat or adapt this list of questions to ask your stepchildren.

1. How did your family celebrate birthdays?
2. Who was responsible for indoor tasks such as laundry, cooking, vacuuming, and organization?

3. How did your family view travel and other experiences that created memories?

4. What types of things happened when a member of your family broke a rule or did not fulfill his or her end of a bargain?

5. Who was responsible for the family finances, and how did your family view spending and saving money?

The process of redefining new expectations can lead children to feel lost, insecure, and confused about their own identity. It makes sense to approach building your blended family with a clean slate. The problem that children have with this approach is that cleaning their slate means confusing their identity. Children do not have a lifetime of experiences that have helped them shape a secure and confident view of self. Instead, they have a short segment of time to study patterns and roles in their family. In this life stage, family history plays a huge role in shaping not just what they do but who they are. Engage your stepchildren with this list of questions, and continue to add more as your relationship grows. Foster conversation about their personalities, their past family traditions, and their routines and roles. Where you can, incorporate the information you gather from these conversations into the present and future roles and routines of your blended family.

Ultimate Identity Shapers

A 2015 Barna research study revealed, "While many factors make up human self-identity, most Americans agree the primary factor that makes up their identity is family. Nearly two-thirds of Americans say their family makes up 'a lot' of their personal identity (62%)."[2] The second and third factors reported in this research were:

2. Being an American
3. Religious faith

This data is helpful for understanding why children depend so heavily on their family structure to shape their identity, unlike adults, who have had a lifetime of influencing messages to understand and help define theirs. This is one of the reasons some children of divorce have identity struggles.

Earlier in this chapter I referenced that fragmentation I experienced while feeling stuck between being a "first-marriage kid" and an unfamiliar cultural Scottish clan. My maiden name did not fit comfortably into either family culture. I wish I could share a secret formula for healing a broken identity. Full redemptive healing is possible; however, the process is not always quick or guaranteed.

My understanding of "team" was confused by two different family names and symbols. Have you ever been torn as a sports fan? You have ties to both sides, so you are not sure which jersey to wear for the big game-watching party. This metaphor helps to further explain the identity crisis children are experiencing. Children must be willing to find their identity in victory over their circumstances instead of falling victim to the divorce narrative.

How can children find this type of victory?

One of the ways to help children strengthen their identity is by verbalizing and modeling your commitment to them, communicating that you truly care for them and like having them around. Think of a coach. When a player first joins a team, a great coach will verbalize his commitment to the athlete and speak about his or her strengths and how each adds value to the group: "You matter." "You are one of us." "We miss you when you are not around." Once the uniforms are distributed, everyone wears them knowing that they have a place and that they belong. Whether biological parent or stepparent, you need to find opportunities to communicate to all children the specific ways that you are committed to them and the unique value each child brings to your blended family identity.

Children may not spend all their time on the same sideline, but when strong commitments exist on both sides, they know they fit and belong, even when they are not around for every game. As you communicate your commitments—"I'm here for you," "I enjoy spending time with you," "You make our team better"—be intentional about following up with actions that support your words. This investment begins to build identity in the child; it may not materialize until they are much older, but it is important to start the process. The difficult part about commitment on your end is that it may not always be received or reciprocated. Remember to try not to give this too much power, and be assured that your investment is not without dividends, even though they may take longer to materialize.

Another one of the healing agents in resolving the identity crisis following divorce is in their own future marriage. I discuss this fully in a later chapter, but I want to encourage you to grasp the power that covenant and commitment can have in helping children rebuild. When I spoke my wedding vows, I became a Reitsema. With this new name, I had the opportunity to redefine my own nuclear family legacy. Not only did I fully feel like I fit in this family, but I also felt chosen, pursued, and fully known. Starting my own nuclear family provided a fresh start in a role where I maintained the ability to navigate and define my own course.

Taking a new name in marriage brings hopeful change, but claiming a new identity does not require a wedding. For believers, a restored identity is something Scripture outlines when God assigns His followers a new name. When God positioned Abram to be the father of many nations, He changed his name to Abraham: "What's more, I am changing your name. It will no longer be Abram. Instead, you will be called Abraham, for you will be the father of many nations" (Genesis 17:5 NLT).

When God chose Simon as the foundation of His Church, He changed his name to Peter: "Now I say to you that you are Peter (which means 'rock'), and upon this rock I will build my church, and all the powers of hell will not conquer it" (Matthew 16:18 NLT).

One last noteworthy identity change to reference is when Saul, a Jew, began using the Roman translation of his name, Paul, after becoming a follower of Christ. The etymology of his name did not change, but the translation he used did. Saul adopted the Roman translation of his given name to appeal to the Gentiles as a more approachable identity in his outreach mission.[3] The reason this scenario is applicable when understanding redemption of a child's identity after divorce is that it signifies pride in the heritage of Saul's name while still allowing grace to redefine his future legacy.

One of the myths about healing from the divorce identity crisis is that children need to abandon their nuclear family identity and replace it with a new one. As a stepparent, you might even feel pressure to be the change agent for your stepchild's redemptive story. Please note that your stepchildren were born with a family name, and even if that legacy has broken pieces, it is a vital part of who they are. God is the redemptive change agent in rebuilding a stepchild's true identity, and He is sovereign in His process to complete this work in His children.

─────────── CHAPTER 5 ───────────
TAKEAWAY SUMMARY

1. Study former familial roles, allowing freedom to explore where some might be replicable.

2. Embrace your stepchild's fragmented experience. Accept the cracks rather than expecting a brand-new, unbroken picture.

3. Be open and willing to learn about your stepchild's previous family history.

4. Verbalize and demonstrate your unwavering commitment.

5. Allow God to be the one to do the miraculous work of identity restoration.

6

Lingering Effects

It is noble to embrace all children in your blended family as your own; however, giving yourself the freedom to own the fact that milestones are different with your biological children is a fair and honest expectation. Posturing yourself as if there is truly no difference at all carries the risk of feeling fake and fabricated from the child's perspective.

Growing up with four kids under one roof created an environment that was rarely devoid of drama. Most siblings recall scenes involving teasing and tears, tormenting and tattling, or tantrums and time-outs. In the moment, these outbursts are frustrating and emotionally exhausting, but with a little distance and perspective, some of these experiences can be quite comical. My mom had a handful of tricks she employed to help us recapture our smiles during these high-stress sibling spats. One such tactic was something I promised myself I would never repeat in my own parenting, yet its effect was so powerful that I've since recanted my promise and have utilized it with my own kids.

When things became especially dramatic among my siblings, my mom would cue her jazz hands, bounce them side to side in perfect rhythm, and sing a tune with the words, "Hollywood, dah nah-nah-nah-nah-nah-nah, Hollywood, dah nah-nah-nah-nah-nah-nah!" We tried everything to stop the performance— plugging our ears, running to different rooms, or pleading, "Please stop! Seriously, it's not funny!" Our efforts were rarely successful in stopping the song-and-dance routine, and after a few valiant efforts to quell the singing, giggles replaced our grimaces, and the atmosphere in our house returned to one of joy and peace.

As a little girl, I often was the culprit in the dramatic scenes. I was determined, driven, and full of energy. Wisely, my parents channeled my big personality into a children's theater program, where I fell in love with the stage and the opportunity to entertain through acting, music, and dance. My theatrics had a place to shine and planted a dream to one day see my name in Broadway lights. Much of my childhood was spent on stage, auditioning for various roles, celebrating casting victories, and learning to accept rejection when others were chosen instead.

For my thirteenth birthday, my mom and grandma arranged a surprise trip to New York City. The magic of the city captured my heart. We ate falafel from a street cart, meandered through Central Park, hugged giant teddy bears at FAO Schwarz, and played dress-up at the famous Saks Fifth Avenue. By far, the highlight of this milestone birthday weekend was when we took our seats in the Palace Theater to experience the premiere season of *Beauty and the Beast* on stage. My whole heart engaged the opportunity. It felt magical. Even today, I vividly remember the sights, the sounds, the mystery. How did Chip, being a live child actor, float on a saucer without the audience seeing his body or legs? What made it possible for the beast to transform into a real prince without leaving the stage? That weekend was what dreams are made of, and I longed for the opportunity to re-create similar milestone memories when I had a daughter of my own.

Last fall, that very opportunity presented itself. I read that Denver was selected as the city to premiere *Frozen, the Broadway Musical*. The marketing sparked my attention and reminded me of the delight I experienced when my mom and grandmother surprised me with *Beauty and the Beast* tickets. My daughter was the perfect age to appreciate the magic of Disney on stage, and I could not wait to call my mom and propose a plan to reenact history with the next generation. The phone began to ring. My heart was racing with excitement. This was such a fun opportunity—what family legacies are made of. Mom picked up.

"Hey, honey."

"Hi, Mom! I just had the best idea. *Frozen*, the musical, is premiering in Denver, and I'd love to surprise Lia with tickets. We could dress up and go out to dinner beforehand and make a memory like you and Grandma created for me with *Beauty and the Beast* in New York." I anticipated an enthusiastic "Yes!" Instead I heard her say, "I love that idea, but we already bought tickets for Anna and Sarah, and I'm not sure I really want to go twice in one weekend." My heart hit the floor. Anna and Sarah were my stepdad's biological granddaughters—my mom's stepgrandchildren—who were thirteen and twelve. It was a thoughtful and kind gesture to consider this show for them as a birthday present, but because of this decision, I felt robbed of the opportunity to make a sacred memory with my mom. My idea was not even original. It was like someone beat me to the punch and committed to a moment I could never reclaim. I wrestled in my thoughts for a moment. *Would girls*

their age even enjoy Frozen? *Why wasn't my daughter considered when they were purchasing tickets?* I allowed emotional
freedom to process these considerations, then made the decision
to hit redial on my phone. My mom picked up and graciously
listened as I shared my heart.

"Mom, I fully understand the cost and time involved in going
twice to the same musical; however, it is extremely important
for me to have the opportunity to experience milestone memories like this with you and with my daughter. I am going to ask
that you consider coming with us and allowing me to make
a memory that doesn't fall into the shadow of my stepdad's
older granddaughters." Recognizing my process, she lovingly
and enthusiastically arranged to join us and helped me to fulfill my vision for a Broadway musical experience together. We
treasured the show and the time we had together.

Stolen Firsts

What happened in this scenario is a very common lingering effect
of divorce and blended families. I refer to these moments as stolen firsts—life events that follow those of others who have already
gone before you. Instead of making the inaugural march toward
celebratory milestones, you sometimes feel like a shadow or an
afterthought when stepparents and siblings have gone before you.

Thanksgiving Day, 2009, my sister-in-law and I were both
pregnant with our first children. I remember the scene like yes-
terday. My mom and stepdad had hosted a beautiful dinner.
Boisterous conversation flowed, and there was a celebratory
atmosphere in the air. As we cleared our plates and meandered
toward the couch for the football games, my stepdad lovingly
put his arms around my sister-in-law and me and said, "I cannot wait for grandbabies number five and number six. Can you

imagine this house next year with two more precious babies around the table? We are so blessed. I am so excited for you both. We truly have so much to be thankful for." We acknowledged his kind words and took our place in the living room to rest our weary and very pregnant bodies. A few hours later, when Josh and I got in the car, I burst into tears.

"Is everything okay?" Josh inquired. "What's behind those tears?"

"Josh," I began, "these babies are number one and number two. I know he has grandchildren already, but hearing these kids labeled as number five and number six broke my heart. I never realized that, even eleven years after my parents' divorce, I'd be so hurt by these blended family dynamics."

"You know what the best part of this story is?" my husband responded. Admittedly, I did not want him to find light amid my sorrow. Still, it sounded like he was setting up something profound, so I leaned in. "The best part of this story, Lauren, is that this baby will never feel like you are feeling right now." In that moment, Josh offered me much-needed assurance that he was committed to our marriage for the long haul. He wanted to break a pattern of hurt and remind me that I had nothing to fear regarding his intentions with our forever family.

My stepdad was kind, sincere, loving, and celebratory. He did nothing wrong. In fact, from his perspective, he was honoring us by fully embracing these future grandchildren and celebrating them as if they were his own. My heart, however, felt once again burdened by the reality that our rights to forge family firsts had been stolen by a blended family who happened to have experienced having children before I did.

It is important to recognize the difficult position stepparents find themselves navigating when faced with these moments. On one hand, you receive advice about being careful not to favor your biological children over your stepchildren, and on the other hand, when you embrace your stepchildren like one of your own, you discover you have hurt feelings or have done something wrong. Your tender position comes with an equal amount of pressure to do the right thing and make the right call. I want to encourage you as you juggle this role.

My stepdad was not wrong to purchase *Frozen* tickets for his older granddaughters, nor was he malicious in his celebratory comments about my growing family. However, both examples triggered sadness in me and felt unfair. Is there any way to prevent these experiences or lessen the negative feelings stepchildren may have when they occur? The following guidelines are included to help diffuse the potential hurt your stepchildren may feel when stolen firsts manifest as lingering effects of their parents' divorce.

1. List major milestones for each child in your blended family. Make one list for your biological children and one for your stepchildren.

   Milestones are actions or events marking a significant change or stage in development. For children, milestones may include losing a first tooth, attending a first concert or sporting event, or transitioning from elementary school to middle school. In early adolescence—getting braces removed, earning a driver's license, or making a varsity sports team. In adulthood—weddings, job assignments, and new babies.

2. Place each milestone on an appropriate timeline.

3. Highlight the events on your stepchildren's list that you have already experienced with one or more of your biological children.

4. Create a plan for approaching and celebrating the
   highlighted moments from the perspective of a
   "first-timer."

If a do-over were possible for my mom and stepdad with
these guidelines in place, I believe the level of pain and disappointment triggered would have been lessened. Had my
mom recognized my vision and desire for a Broadway musical milestone with her firstborn granddaughter, she would
not have hesitated to go twice. Had my stepdad approached
my first pregnancy without a numbers mentality in his grandchild lineage, I would not have left our Thanksgiving dinner
in tears. Although I appreciated his heart to include my children as additions to his list of grandchildren, had he known
to approach the conversation from a first-time perspective, I
would have felt more celebrated and less resentful. It is noble
to embrace all children in your blended family as your own;
however, giving yourself the freedom to own the fact that milestones are different with your biological children is a fair and
honest expectation. Posturing yourself as if there is truly no
difference at all carries the risk of feeling fake and fabricated
from the child's perspective.

Stolen firsts not only affect stepchildren but are also common for stepparents to experience. A friend recently shared a
conversation reflecting on the emotional process she experienced when marrying her husband, Jeff, who had a son prior to
meeting her. She described the early years after the wedding: "I
felt like I was borrowing someone else's life." Her words were
profound and provided the context to further build empathy
from the stepparent perspective. She described how after the
wedding, when she moved into their new home, nothing felt
safe to change. The house previously had been occupied by a

father-and-son duo who had roots and memories in each part of the house. Room décor was established and routines were in place. She had a vision for her own space, desiring a voice in everything from curtain fabric choice to cabinet organization in the kitchen. But she was sensitive to her young stepson's routine.

Jacob was beginning kindergarten in the fall, his dad was now married, and his biological mom had recently moved to a new house. With all the transition in his world, the last thing she wanted to do was add more change. Her life, on the other hand, had changes of its own, but the sensitivity to her stepson's process outweighed, from her perspective, an interior decorating shift. My friend had never been married before. This was her first wedding, her first husband, and their first home as a couple, yet she sacrificed her right to *firsts* to honor the difficult and tender transition process for her stepson.

"I remember sitting on the couch with Jeff, and Jacob would climb in between us and wedge himself into a perfect family cuddle spot. My reaction surprised me. I wasn't upset that Jacob was there, but for the first time it hit me—I was not going to be able to have the alone time as a couple that I had envisioned for my marriage." Many people are aware of children's grief after remarriage, but some may miss that grief is also shared by the adults. If you have experienced stolen firsts in your stepparent role, allow yourself the freedom and the safety to express them with your spouse. Take time to communicate what you had envisioned and to express any disappointments that may accompany your circumstances. It is important for stepchildren and parents to be honest in owning the emotions that partner stolen firsts.

Back to my story about the *Frozen* musical tickets: Had I not called my mom back and verbalized my sadness about the situation, I might have buried that memory as further resentment toward not only her, but also toward my stepdad. Buying the tickets and going to the show after a hard conversation was not my ideal vision, but it offered both sides a second chance to do what was within our power to redeem that dream. Recognize which situations are within your power to change and which ones you cannot. In the example I shared about Jacob interrupting a quiet, newlywed snuggle scene on the couch, expecting Jacob not to be in their house was unrealistic. Although she and Jeff could not reset their marriage firsts to exclude this beloved little boy, as a couple they did have the power to express the emotional reaction when the interruption occurred and begin dialogue about healthy boundaries for protecting alone time. *What could that look like? When was it most likely to happen? What types of conversations needed to happen with Jacob to communicate some new family boundaries? How would the couple share this change with Jacob?*

Just as I had to make an effort to pick up the phone and ask my mom for a second look at the offer to join us for the play, you have the option to look at how stolen firsts affect you emotionally, doing your best to be open about what you might need to diffuse the pain-points. Many stepparents I've talked with say communicating more of their needs often engenders guilt. *I'm the adult. This is much more difficult for the children, so I will be the one to sacrifice and ensure I don't further rock the boat.* These sentiments are thoughtful and kind, but without the emotional safety to honestly identify and process your own disappointments, you put yourself and your marriage at greater risk for future strife. Unspoken disappointments root resentment and bitterness, sentiments that can devastate relationships if unresolved.

(Step)parentification

Another lingering effect experienced by children of divorce in a blended family structure is the heavy pressure they feel to be sensitive toward, and responsible for, the emotional well-being of their stepparents. Sometimes there is a perception that your stepchildren intentionally aim to hurt you. In my experience, this is not the thought process. I remember a conversation I had with my dad a few days after my stepmom's birthday had come and gone. He shared frustration about the lack of acknowledgment or care she felt after checking the mailbox to discover there was no card from me. The same hurt ensued on Mother's Day. Why didn't his daughter have the decency to recognize her stepmom and make her feel celebrated? It is one day of the year, and it is something I should easily remember.

As I processed the phone call later that day, I felt overwhelmed. Was it not enough to verbalize or express my appreciation for the role she played in my life? Guilt hit first. Once again, I was the cause of my stepmom's pain. I should have remembered to run to the store and get something in the mail. After the guilt came frustration. I wanted the freedom to know that not sending a birthday card was not indicative of my heart toward my stepmother. After frustration, I felt overwhelmed. How am I supposed to balance making everyone in my blended family feel cared for in a meaningful way? So I did a little blended-family-tree exercise.

I took a piece of scratch paper and began to make a list of all the immediate family members I had. This list included all the immediate family members on both of my stepfamily sides as well as the immediate family members on my husband's side. I wrote only the names of siblings and parents on both sides. After completing the list, I counted twenty-one names. Yes, twenty-one. That did not include my own kids or any of my nieces and nephews. At this moment, I had a realization. I am not only expected to remember one day of the year; I am expected to remember twenty-one. And if I felt compelled to send a card to one person, I had to be sensitive to remember that gesture for every additional blended family member so as to not create the appearance of preference. Suddenly, I felt a lot of pressure. As a working mom, with children of my own, a community of friendships to nurture, and twenty-one family members, I was sure to let a lot of people down—and regularly.

Now I am an adult, but when my parents remarried, I was a teenager. From the beginning, I recall conversations I had with both parents about my attitude, my expressions, the things I said (or failed to say), and how these attitudes and actions were negatively received by my stepmom and my stepdad. I was expected to be selfless, gracious, kind, and sensitive to the feelings of adults during my own selfish developmental growth. A journal posted by experts at Compass Rose Academy, a residential treatment facility for adolescent girls ages fourteen to eighteen, explains: "The reason teenagers act selfishly could be because of the way their brains operate. According to a study by University College London, teenagers hardly use the area of the brain that considers other people's emotions and thoughts when making a decision. They are even less likely to consider their own emotions than adults do."[1]

This stress, the pressure to tend to and care for the emotional well-being of parents, has been labeled by researchers as *parentification*. Cindy Lamothe, a contributor for the *Washington Post*, wrote in an article titled "Your Child Is Not Your Confidant":

Experts believe this kind of behavior [depending on children to care for emotional needs of a parent] creates an atmosphere of neglect, because children are made responsible for looking after the emotional and psychological well-being of the parent while suppressing their normal childhood needs, such as play or friendships with kids their own age.

. . . When a child starts serving as a friend to the parent, and the parent is getting his or her needs met through the child— that becomes problematic.[2]

I recognized my parents' desire to protect their new spouses from being the target of attitudinal disrespect from a teenager, but I believe I had not yet developed the brain pathways to approach my stepparents from a posture of selflessness. The expectation that I do so, however, followed me through adulthood, leaving me feeling pressured to consider my stepparents' emotional well-being during many of my own milestones. When I graduated from college, I worried about how many pictures I should plan to take with each side after the ceremony. On my wedding day, I was nervous about who would sit where, when each side would participate in my pre-ceremonial festivities, and how to arrange each family member at the reception. When I had my first baby, I needed to make sure everyone was invited to the hospital, but I also wanted to be sensitive to giving each person access to the baby in a way that made him or her feel special and appreciated. I believe there is some part of parentification that can translate in stepparent relationships.

(Step)parentification can be a lingering effect after divorce. While stepchildren should be experiencing the emotional freedom to enjoy life's biggest milestones, they often are preoccupied with stress surrounding their actions and the effect they have on a stepparent's feelings. No child or adolescent should use this idea as an excuse to dishonor or disrespect stepparents, but better understanding of the emotional stress stepchildren carry in trying to please stepparents can offer an important perspective on the struggle.

How can stepparents cope with some of the hurt and disrespect they feel from their stepchildren?

1. **Find your emotional safety in truth, in your spouse, and in your adult friendships.** God's truth tells us: "I have loved you, my people, with an everlasting love. With unfailing love I have drawn you to myself" (Jeremiah 31:3 NLT). Remember, above all, that Christ's love is the only complete love that will fulfill your heart in confidence. Seek Christ to refresh your spirit, as your stepchildren can easily drain it. Second to God's love for you, trust in and nurture the love you have for your spouse. Be careful not to ask your spouse to choose or weigh their love between you and their children. Instead, trust them to allow God's abundant love to be enough for both dimensions of your family. Lastly, surround yourself with an authentic community of adults rather than seeking from your stepchildren the approval or support your heart needs.

2. **Recognize the number of people who expect attention and affirmation from the children.** When parents remarry after divorce, they no longer play an emotionally supportive role for their prior spouse. Children, on the other hand, acquire new emotional responsibilities for an extended group of people. Give grace where you can, as they are working to juggle the expectations of an expansive number of family members.

3. **Trust positive deposits.** When your stepchildren say or do something that honors you, write it down and believe it. It is always nice to be reminded of the things they

appreciate about you, but if the expectation is that they consistently offer more, you might find yourself disappointed. It is easier for people to remember negative experiences than the positive ones. This idea is validated through the research of Drs. Howard Markman, Scott Stanley, and Susan Blumberg. Their studies "highlight the fact that negative beliefs and interpretations can powerfully filter out the positive and leave one seeing only the negative."[3] Because it is a natural tendency to remember the negative more easily, we have to be intentional and disciplined about recording and recollecting the positive. It is unrealistic that every stepchild's word, action, or behavior toward you is negative, but research does prove that we can confidently expect the negative to outweigh the positive. Prepare your heart and mind to combat this reality by committing to track and trust any positive and encouraging moments you experience in your relationship with your stepchildren. Consider capturing these sentiments in writing and putting them somewhere you will see them regularly. This way, you will be better equipped to believe the positive deposits when negativity strikes.

CHAPTER 6
TAKEAWAY SUMMARY

1. Recognize the reality of stolen firsts. Be intentional in allowing each child to experience his or her own milestones as a star rather than as a shadow.

2. Consider the heavy weight children often carry when trying to navigate adults' emotions. Remember to keep to your role as a

parent and allow them to keep to their role as children. Helpful tips to avoid the effects of (step)parentification:

a. Find your emotional safety in truth, in your spouse, and in your adult friendships.

b. Recognize the number of people who expect attention and affirmation from the children and have empathy for the amount of emotional energy that is expected.

c. Trust the positive deposits, thus giving less power to the negative ones.

7

Receiving Love

It is impossible to duplicate intimate moments with sincerity. You can learn the details and recapture some of the story's highlights, but nothing compares to firsthand experience.

My work sometimes involves traveling, and typically in these scenarios my packing list is composed of business casual selections that withstand suitcase stacking with the least number of wrinkles. Each summer, I get to go on one trip where I exchange my business casual attire for a suitcase full of sweatshirts, jeans, cotton T-shirts, and Chacos. This type of travel is not for work, but rather as a volunteer for an organization that invests in the lives of teenagers. My area of influence is with the sixth- through eighth-graders. Some might say that traveling to a property on a charter bus filled with Pringles-popping, selfie-snapping, prepubescent tweens is not an appropriate setting for a thirty-something mother of two with a full-time job; however, from my perspective, this week is better than any vacation. I get to sleep in cabin bunks with sixteen young ladies, many of whom have never been away from home for consecutive nights before, and engage with them in epic adventures.

Throughout this week, I sit in the company of kids who are becoming young adults and am trusted with their life's greatest joys. Amidst the joy, I often hear them risk vulnerability for the first time as they process and verbalize some of their hardships. I do not invest as a leader for these young ladies for a paycheck or for a pat on the back. It's because I can help someone just like someone helped me.

My freshman year of high school, I was one of the young people someone invited to join the crew for a twenty-four-hour bus ride to a gorgeous lake property in Minnesota. The invitation came at a pivotal time when I was in the midst of my parents' divorce. My leader gave up time with her family to come hear about mine, and that forever changed me. The week was packed with exhilarating events—a quarter-mile zip line into the water, parasailing with my closest friends, relaxing in a hot tub built for fifty, and incredible food. For me, the most precious part of the experience was not in the energy or adventure of all the fun, but rather in the sacred space where we gathered with our leader to share life. This experience modeled intimacy.

During the week, I learned that my leader had also grown up in a family that experienced a divorce. Her empathetic and compassionate posture allowed me the freedom to process everything in a safe space, and better yet, as an adult, she shared some of the healing and hope that was ahead of me. I am still in touch with my leader today. More than twenty years have transpired since I stepped on a charter bus for that journey to Pelican Lake, but the legacy of the week remains fresh.

My most recent trip with my middle-school crew was unique, as I was five months' pregnant with my third baby. Although having a baby on board did not drastically change the experience, it did call for a few adjustments. I had to sit out some of the activities, and when it came time for bed, I was a little less lenient on the late-night whispers and teenage giggles that I typically would have allowed after lights-out. A pregnant woman needs her sleep! Although sitting on the sidelines for the giant pendulum swing and the cabin pyramid challenge didn't change my love for the girls, I noticed it slightly shifted the dynamic I was accustomed to experiencing with my cabin. After each activity that pregnancy prevented me from participating in, the girls chose to engage more candidly with our student leaders than with me. I authentically was interested in hearing about what had happened, and I truly wanted to encourage and affirm each of the campers for taking risks and going for it. Yet, because I did not participate, the girls felt closer to the leaders who were actually doing the activity with them. By sharing the experience together, there was a sense of connection and camaraderie that could not be replicated by telling me about it.

In order to fully know their experience, I had to be there, participating in and experiencing the event live and in action. Have you ever walked in on a group right as they were sharing a laugh over a memory they recalled together? With interest and a desire to engage, the bystander often asks, "What's all the laughter about?" Sometimes one of the participants begins to repeat the story, but words fall flat and just don't do justice in summarizing the experience. Typically, this scenario ends with one or more people saying, "You had to be there." It is impossible to duplicate intimate moments with sincerity. You can learn the details and recapture some of the story's highlights, but nothing compares to firsthand experience.

One of the best gifts in relationships is the intimacy that comes with being witness to the everyday happenings in the life of someone you care about. Intimacy is a part of relationships that people have miscategorized as only the physical connection between romantic partners, but true intimacy happens in many of our close relationships—with family members, children, friends, and especially with Christ. One of the ways we can better (and memorably) define intimacy is by viewing and saying it as *into me see*. We have true intimacy in our relationships when we let other people see parts of our lives, our hearts, our emotions, our pain, and our thoughts that we do not share with just anyone. What is so unique and special about *into me see* (intimacy) is that each of us experiences it only with a select number of people. By its very nature, intimacy with too many people dilutes its power and purpose in our connections. If I experienced the same level of intimacy with the person scanning my groceries in the checkout lane as I did with my husband or children, it would signal a major breach of conduct when it comes to personal boundaries. It is important to protect intimacy among a close and small group of people; otherwise, its bonding power weakens.

Few people would argue against the expectation to keep your most personal stories and secrets for your spouse or best friend; however, a different set of rules applies to love, which, we are taught, is for all people to express to one another. Sometimes we can experience love very genuinely, but when its context is not an intimate relationship, people may miss, sometimes entirely, the expression of love being offered. This mindset is one I feel can cause a lot of hurt and misunderstanding between stepchildren and stepparents. Stepparents offer love to a child and hope or expect to receive it back. How love is reciprocated, however, often is not expressed in an intimate way, and therefore is missed or perceived as rejection by stepparents. This can leave them doubting that love even exists and can cause hurts and frustrations that run deep in a stepparent's heart.

Desiring and expecting love from your stepchildren is understandable. Love is something all people need, desire, and expect, regardless of any familial role. Think about how often love appears in slogans or on signposts as the solution to the broken parts of our world: Love conquers all. All you need is love. Love wins. For believers, love is the most important and compelling motivation and instruction composing the entire gospel narrative:

- "For God so loved the world that he gave his one and only Son" (John 3:16).
- "Whoever does not love does not know God, because God is love" (1 John 4:8).
- "A new command I give you: Love one another" (John 13:34).

Love truly is the most important thing. Love matters. Love, however, is different from intimacy. I believe that differentiating between the two can help mitigate some of the pain stepparents feel when their attempts to express love feel shut down. Additionally, I will share three barriers that act as a wall in a stepchild's heart that sometimes prevent them from fully opening up to receive the love being offered.

Distinguish Between Love and Intimacy

Have you ever felt as though your stepchildren love the stepparent on the other side more than they love you? Has this perception been one that frustrates your heart and begs the question,

Why? For a participant in one of my conference workshops, this was an ever-present struggle in his blended family experience. The gentleman asked for perspective about his experience with his two biological children: "Why do both kids love my former wife and her new husband so much but treat us like garbage? We do everything for them, and ironically, parents who do nothing are doted on like heroes."

As I pursued a few contextual details, I learned that these parents were the primary caretakers for both children, providing a majority of, if not all, the financial support, consistency in schedule and discipline, and faith foundation. Even though the former wife was the parent who had left the family in the first place, the children appeared to display more love and acceptance toward her and her new spouse.

This common scenario is one that can be better understood by differentiating between love and intimacy. Love takes less risk with people you see infrequently or who have limited exposure to your everyday experience. When time spent with one side of the family is in a vacation setting and only occurs a couple of times a year, there is much less risk and exposure for intimacy. Love feels natural, as there is only fun to be had to maximize the impact of these visits. Intimacy, however, is not as present or deep in these situations. To cultivate authentic intimacy in relationship, presence and exposure are imperative.

I have never met the children in this family but can assume (from the data provided) that they have achieved a significant degree of intimacy with the father and stepmother. Intimacy, however, is not being expressed in loving behaviors. Instead, these parents are experiencing more of the pain and struggle shared through intimate relationship than they are seeing the joyful love experience that comes after healing. Rather than viewing their kids as being more loving toward the other side, I might challenge them to adopt a new perspective: Be willing to see the rich intimacy offered through presence and experience, and take heart in knowing that after the struggle often comes rich reward.

Becoming pregnant with our third child was incredibly difficult. My husband and I routinely pictured a large family together and were open to growing our family after our young son turned one. We never could have imagined the struggle we would have in trying to accomplish this. Four years went by with no evidence that our family would ever grow. We had nearly given up hope and were almost resigned to alternative options for seeing our dream come true when we received the great surprise of a positive pregnancy test. We were elated. This news came right before a family trip we had planned to Disney World with some of our closest friends. Josh and I conspired over the perfect plan to let our kids in on the news that their dream of being older siblings was finally coming true. We decided to capitalize on the magical world of Disney and share the news through a princess visit with Tinker Bell.

We waited in line, anticipating the reaction we would see when the famous fairy revealed our secret. Our friends stood in line ahead of us, and before leaving their photo session, they whispered the plan into Tink's ear: "When this next family comes to grab a photo, would you be willing to tell the kids a special surprise? Their mom is going to have a baby, and we would love your help in creating this significant memory." Tinker Bell, albeit a bit nervous, was all in to help us. We snapped a picture with Peter Pan's sidekick, and before moving on to the next family in line, the fairy princess knelt and whispered to our kids, "Thank you so much for visiting me today. Before you leave, I wanted to share a magical secret that

I learned about in Pixie Hollow. It sounds like you are going to be a big sister and big brother soon. Your mom is having a baby!" Both digested the announcement and looked to Josh and me for confirmation.

"You're having a baby?" Lia asked.

"We are!" I answered. The kids ran toward us with delight and embraced us in a tight group hug. That night the celebration continued as we watched the fireworks explode behind Cinderella's castle and listened to the fitting lyrics of "When You Wish Upon a Star." We danced with glow sticks and embraced one another. The magic of Disney did not disappoint, yet the real magic was in the heart of our Creator, who had graciously given our family the desires of our heart. I went back to our hotel that night and journaled:

Heavenly Father, thank you does not do justice to express our gratitude for this indescribable gift. You truly see us, and you have been so faithful in our waiting. Please do not let me be one of the ten who forgets to come back to you and give thanks for what you have done. We delight in your promise and cannot wait for what is to come.

We returned from our epic family vacation and began sharing the news with family and friends who had prayed with us along the way. Ten days later, I was in the mountains preparing for a breakout session I was teaching to a group of college students. I woke up early, and something physically triggered concern. My concerns were soon validated after visiting the doctor with my husband to learn that we had lost the baby. Our hearts plummeted in disbelief and despair. How could this be happening? This was not supposed to be the way this story ended. Yet there was no escaping our stolen dream. One of the most difficult parts was sharing the news with our children. They, too, were devastated.

This season was extremely intimate for us as a family and for my heart toward God. Did we love one another any less? Not at all. Did we feel less love from or toward God? I definitely wrestled with questions, wondering why such a precious gift was taken after such an epic celebration. Yet in the wrestling, hurt, and pain, I sat in the midst of deep intimacy with my Savior. He knew my heart and its struggles and disappointments. I was angry and felt teased. At times I neglected talking to Him completely. My heart was too raw to come close. I needed His love, yet I was desperate to protect my heart from further disappointment. I did not know what to ask for or how to pray. My posture was sad, and I felt robbed of something I desperately thought He would fix.

In the midst of my brokenhearted process, I may not have felt the abounding love I knew was in His character, yet I was deeply intimate with Him. Jesus was not distant; He was right smack in the middle of my process. Yes, I distanced myself, but this distance did not negate my love. My spirit needed time, and eventually, when my heart felt ready, I began to take steps to approach Him again—to speak truth about His character, and to express my heart's gratitude and affection for the role He occupied in my life.

Does this emotional cycle sound familiar in your experience of feeling cut out or flat-out rejected by your stepchildren? You posture yourself to be interested in their story, present in their circumstances, and supportive in their process, yet all you seem to get in response is attitude, pushback, distance, and disrespect? Meanwhile, it can feel like those who are not present at all, or who act as the "Disney World parents," without rules or hardship, get all the love. I imagine how unfair this must feel. I bet it feels a lot like how God might have felt when He could see the bigger plan unfold and wanted my love and trust as He worked out the details. Instead, all He got from me in my deepest disappointment was distance.

Be encouraged that the posture you see in your stepchildren, or sometimes even in your biological children, is actually quite intimate. They are letting you see into their pain. Granted, this picture, especially in early adolescence, feels like the antithesis of intimacy. It feels like war—a personal attack against you that is designed and planned to sting. Take heart, and remember the words from chapter 4, "It's Not About You." Consider the grace in being witness to their struggle. Allow them the space each needs to grieve their own disappointments. Remind yourself that your love for them is not in vain. Kids cannot reject forever those who love them well; however, your stepchildren may not always have the words or capacity to express their love in intimate ways.

The Stress of Duplication

A few months ago I picked my daughter up from her grandma's house after school and was excited to see her and get a recap of her day. My after-school questions were familiar to her, as I am accustomed to spouting off the same list almost daily. Typically, I would have picked her up from school, but on this particular day, her grandma covered carpool and brought her over to her house for a few hours before I arrived.

When I picked her up, we loaded into the car and I checked the rearview mirror, confirming that she was buckled in, then began my great inquisition. "What was the best part of your day, sweetie? Did you enjoy your lunch?" Her answers were short, and I sensed an attitude brewing in her tone. After only the second question, she snapped, "I don't want to talk about it." *Wow*, I thought. Something hard must have happened. In true Mom fashion I began to dig with even more questions.

"Oh, honey, is everything okay? Was someone mean to you? Did your teacher say something that made you feel embarrassed?" Determined to get to the bottom of what had turned my tenderhearted, communicative daughter into a rude, short-tempered child, I probed with every intent to fix it. Her answer was so telling.

"Mom, nothing bad happened. Grandma already asked me all these questions, and I just don't like repeating myself." Her words struck me with such clarity. I am the same way. After a while, the details of my life just don't feel as meaningful or sincere when I have to repeat myself. I gave her the emotional space to be off-duty for my after-school interview. That afternoon, Grandma got to be the recipient of Lia's emotional check-in, and Lia was out of gas to duplicate the authenticity and excitement she had already shared.

As I processed this conversation later, I recognized some parallel sentiments in a child's experience as part of a blended family. When children split their time between family members, they are routinely required to report the play-by-play of what happened in their life prior to their arrival. If the parental switch happens on a weekend, they often are greeted with, "How was your week? Did anything fun happen at school? Your mom (or dad) was telling me about a big assignment you are working on. Is there anything we can do to help its progress?" Although the questions are perfectly acceptable and asked without malicious intent, there is risk of these questions being answered with attitude. Why? Because the children have already given the play-by-play once, and the second time is frustrating and can feel annoying.

It is already difficult to get authentic and honest conversation out of a child, but to expect that child to have the capacity and grace to duplicate their life experience so that both sides of the blended family have equal access to the full story can be an unfair expectation. One of the sacrifices parents must accept as part of a blended family is that they may need to surrender their need or right to know all the details of a child's experience. It is important to offer space to create authentic and memorable moments during your time together rather than working to summarize a detailed narrative from the other side. Keep this in mind during your next attempt to engage your children and stepchildren in genuine conversation about something they have previously shared with the other parent or stepparent. Your attempts to pursue their heart may be met with more resistance than expected.

Subconscious Guilt

I find it very interesting to watch children learn to navigate different social settings. The summer months often take on a life of their own. Kids who interact every day in the same classes at school might see one another at the swimming pool and completely ignore each other. Close friends who are inseparable on a playdate might see each other at the grocery store with another neighbor or friend and walk by as if they didn't notice one another. I have seen this pattern unfold a few times, not only with my own children in their social groups, but also among the middle school kids I spend time with regularly in our community. Wanting to discern their thought process, I recently approached one of the girls I witnessed blatantly ignoring a friend during a chance encounter at the local library.

"Hey, Caitlyn," I greeted her. "I'm just curious about why, when you saw Michelle the other day at the library, you kind of ignored her. Are you guys not getting along?"

"We're great!" she answered. "We're definitely not fighting right now. I just saw that she was there with one of her friends from her neighborhood and didn't want to get in the way of their time together," she explained. I found it odd, but profound, that she was aware of another person's perceived jealousy for interrupting a social encounter that did not originally include her. In a way, Caitlyn felt that saying hi to one of her closest friends was not allowable in this particular social setting. After hearing her perspective, I offered her assurance that it is always permissible to care for and honor friends beyond the one you are with in that moment. A friend who is secure in his or her relationships should never feel jealous or angry if another person also expresses care and concern for that friend. This explanation is one that can be applied as stepchildren navigate appropriate social boundaries with their stepparents.

Sometimes children feel that giving or receiving love from someone who is not their biological parent communicates betrayal. By showing the stepparent love and affection, it feels as though they are dishonoring the value or worth of the relationship they have with their parents. Sometimes a biological parent really does feel anger about their child giving some of their heart to the spouse of the ex. Many times there appears to be a double standard in the heart of a biological parent regarding their children's right to affirm and love a stepparent. Often this happens when one parent stays single and the other remarries ahead of him or her. It is important to release your children to express care and affection for each stepparent. It is unfair of a parent to desire that their new partner receive love and affection from their biological children while hoping it will not be offered to or reciprocated by the other biological parent's blended family. Be aware that children already feel a bit of subconscious guilt for allowing genuine feelings to develop for their stepparents. Be careful to ensure you do not, either intentionally or unintentionally, communicate that it is not okay for your children to bond with the new members in the blended family.

Fragile Trust

The final pattern that keeps stepchildren from fully embracing the love offered by their stepparents is the lengthy timeline required to fully establish trust. When a divorce occurs, children experience firsthand the result of broken trust. Even if danger signs are present in a marriage, kids normally believe that their family is supposed to be together. They are still experiencing a season of innocence in their childhood, and until that innocence is lost, children feel secure in trusting that they are loved and that their parents love one another. After a divorce occurs, a guard goes up, and trust is no longer a default posture but rather something that needs to be earned. There is risk in allowing someone else in after you have been hurt. What if this person ends up leaving too? All the effort and work that go into rebuilding a healthy bond and connection a second time could end with yet another round of grief and sense of abandonment.

Many of us walk through a similar process after experiencing our first breakup. In the innocence stage of dating, people rarely consider the heart damage that might come if this seemingly perfect match leaves them. Instead, they succumb to the deeply rooted feelings that create goose bumps and butterflies at just the thought of this person's presence. Trust seems to be a natural response, which does not require a lot of thought.

This person loves you and would never do anything to hurt you. Endorphins cloud your ability to be discerning or protective of your heart. After all, how could someone who makes you this happy ever break your heart? Those of us who have experienced heartache after a breakup we never saw coming are not as open to offering trust blindly the second time around. Instead, we feel fragile and watch closely the patterns of the next person we choose to give access to our heart. We are cautious, and sometimes even fearful, of trying again at all. Whoever comes next has a much more difficult path to receiving our love and affection. Consider this perspective in your quest to earn the affection of your stepchildren. They have experienced one of a family's most difficult breakup stories, and the healing that must occur to rebuild a foundation for connection does not happen overnight.

As you give the stepchildren time to come around, also consider how you communicate "I love you." Both of my stepparents were quite forward and vocal about their love for us. The timing in which they said it and the justifications with which they defended it at first did not feel completely sincere. Saying "I love you" is a big deal, and without providing the time to develop and grow that love, stepparents run the risk that the words will fall on deaf ears. Additionally, the words "I love you" are often justified by stepparents as being somewhat of a package deal with their feelings for the child's biological parent: "I love your mom (or dad) so much, and you are a big part of who they are. I truly love you because I sincerely love your parent." In discussing how love is shared with kids in a stepchild role, this sentiment appears to be consistent. But while it makes logical sense, children do not always find this reasoning convincing. Children maintain their own unique identity and are not necessarily convinced that love for them simply comes attached to love for their parents. Approach each stepchild as an individual, and allow love to develop uniquely and incrementally rather than attaching your affection for the kids to the affection for their parent.

--- CHAPTER 7 ---
TAKEAWAY SUMMARY

1. Recognize the difference between love and intimacy, and allow space and time for both to develop. Wanting to be close and feeling close are different parts of the relationship journey. Allow space and time for feelings of love to catch up with the decision to love.

2. Be aware of the stress and exhaustion children feel when trying to live authentically in two places. Extend grace and accept the parts of life a child chooses to share, recognizing that the circumstances they are living in sometimes prohibit the ability for one or both parents to know their child's whole experience.

3. Some of the pushback you experience in your stepchildren's posture may be due to subconscious guilt they feel for opening up toward you. They may not want to hurt their biological parent and sense that a strong relationship with a stepparent might do so. Be sensitive to this reality as you work to build your connection.

4. After children have watched brokenness in a prior marriage, rarely are they quick to trust that yours will last. Trust requires space, consistency, and time. Allow for each in your bonding process.

8

The Great Wall of Pride

Divorce threatens a family's pride, and to mediate the fall, parents sometimes share their reasons and justifications with their new spouses. The narrative you hear can sometimes further the tension between you and your stepchildren.

Kids ask the best questions. Sometimes they are funny, sometimes they are surprising, and sometimes they challenge you. When approached with such questions, I like to think I have the wisdom and life experience to share an answer that brings clarity, and credentials me as a credible source. One of my favorite question-and-answer exchanges happened when my son was three. During the Christmas season, we were at a restaurant, and our server was short with us and visibly annoyed by many of our requests. My son questioned, "Mom, why is he mad?" Unfortunately, I did not have an answer to his question. My three-year-old took it upon himself to draw his own conclusion and answered by saying, "He probably doesn't have the

Christmas spirit." If you're a parent, you've likely been asked similar questions. In the early days, the questions are basic.

"Mom, how do you spell tree?"

"T-R-E-E."

"Thank you!"

"No problem, honey. Let me know if you need anything else." Something about having the right answer affirms a quiet pride within you—not the kind of boastful, arrogant pride rooted in insecurities, but rather the reassuring confidence of knowing you are needed and have something genuine to offer those you love. Being known and safe in relationships requires the freedom to ask questions without the fear of feeling stupid or less than.

Pride often gets a bad rap as a character flaw. When you picture a prideful person, you probably imagine a know-it-all. Instead of anticipating a healthy conversation, you prepare for an argument and posture yourself to be labeled as wrong. This kind of pride is not productive or healthy in interpersonal relationships. It creates barriers rather than connections, and threatens the opportunity for intimacy. Usually when I detect this type of pride, I suspect a cover-up. The person with whom you are engaging is fearful of revealing his or her shortcomings. They do not want you to find out that they might not know the answer to what you are asking, and often, knowing answers is how they determine their worth.

This pride I am describing is something I wrestle with myself. I am fiercely competitive and love to win. When I try something new, I care about how I perform, and I usually calculate my competency level before even attempting it. If I fear I won't succeed, I sometimes avoid the task entirely.

Before divorce, my family used to camp on the beaches of Lake McConaughy every summer with friends from our church.

Camping with family was always a treasured childhood memory, but camping with friends took the excitement to a new level. Community camping expanded the possibilities for adventure. We could count on the Joneses to bring a boat, the Adamses to haul their Jet Skis, and the Woodses to provide the kayaks. Combined lake toys were just the beginning of community camping benefits. Meals were far from ordinary. Everyone perfected their favorite family recipe and learned to prepare it in bulk on a camp stove. We ate better on the shores of a lake than we did at home in our fancy industrial kitchen. The savory meals nourished us for the sun-soaked activity of each day.

One such activity tested my pride and showcased my drive for victory, no matter what the cost—slalom skiing. Our family did not have experience with boats. (I remember learning to never own a boat, but to always make a friend who does.) We forged a friendship with a boat-owning family who had all the toys—water skis, wakeboards, and tubes. More important than the toys they owned was their generous and patient spirit. They captained that speedboat with such grace and taxied person after person on trips around the cove until each had exposure to, and success with, water sports.

Prior to this experience, I had only been water-skiing one time. When I was ten, my mom set up a lesson on a trip to Florida while visiting my grandparents. I learned the basics and remembered what it felt like to allow the boat to pull me up. By the next year's camping vacation, I was ready for a second attempt.

Rusty was the eldest son of our boat-owning friends and the driver chosen to taxi kids and teach them. I waited in line at the dock for my turn.

"Hop in," he instructed as he dropped off the skiers from the first group. Five of us hurried to select our seat on the white leather bench and zipped our life jackets for a safety check. The kids had settled in for the ride when Rusty's dad came aboard. He took the driver's seat, and Rusty grabbed a ski from the boat storage. I offered to grab his second ski and reached to the bottom of the storage compartment, but Rusty stopped me. "Thanks, Lauren, but I'm good. I don't need another ski. I'm going to slalom." He squeezed a small drop of dish soap into the two rubber boots and tightened the laces to support his ankles. I was intrigued. I had never heard of slalom skiing before. Rusty stepped onto the platform at the back of the boat and gracefully hopped into the water. He tightened his grip on the rope handle and steadied his ski. I watched intently as he let the boat drag and straighten the rope slack.

"Hit it!" he shouted, signaling his dad to kick the motor into gear and accelerate. Up from the water Rusty rose. I watched him cut the wake and carve turns on the glassy surface with a tail of water arching off his ski and glistening in the sun. *Wow*, I remember thinking. *I want to try that kind of water-skiing.* After demonstrating his talent, Rusty signaled his dad to cut the engine, and he slowly sank below the water's surface. His hair was still dry as he swam back to board the boat. I leaned over the edge of my seat and asked, "Can I try one ski?"

"Sure," he responded. "I'm happy to let you try!" As an eleven-year-old, my tiny feet were not suited for the slalom ski boots, so Rusty's approach was to let the boat pull me up on two skis, and then I'd drop a ski and balance into slalom form. It sounded simple enough—yet the task proved quite difficult. I remember waiting for what seemed like the right timing to pull my foot out of a ski and proceed to balance it behind my foot on the other, all while being pulled at top speed to maintain momentum. It was as much a battle in my mind as it was with my body. Even when I felt ready, fear gripped my heart, and I hesitated to commit. Rusty patiently coached me through the steps.

It sounded easy enough, but the process tested every ounce of my strength, endurance, and attitude. I must have attempted to drop a ski more than twenty-five times that afternoon, inevitably losing balance, wiggling atop the water's surface, and crashing face-first behind the boat. Eventually I ran out of time, and my coach ran out of steam. We returned to shore for dinner. I felt frustrated and embarrassed. I knew I could do it and was hungry to prove it to myself and to my boat driver. Feeling deflated, I stopped to fuel my tired muscles with a delicious dinner. I was making my way to the buffet line of pastries when Rusty tapped me on the shoulder.

"The sun's still out for just a little longer. Do you want to try one more time?" Recharged with food and inspired by his tenacious spirit, I replied with an emphatic "Yes!" A few attempts into our dusk boating adventure, I successfully dropped a ski, maintained balance, and felt the thrill of cutting across the wake.

I was beaming with pride. In that moment, the motive behind my pride shifted. At first I had felt prideful to cover up my insecurity, not wanting anyone to see me fail. However, after tasting success, I felt pride well up as a response to victory. Rusty shared in the pride I felt that night—the quiet pride of accomplishment and teamwork, discipline and dedication, patience and persistence. I will never forget Rusty's commitment to helping me succeed. Every time I slalom ski as an adult, I remember the fight I endured to accomplish this goal. Even after we came back to shore and shared the joy of victory with the others, only Rusty could truly understand what it took to succeed, because he was the one who was there to experience this memory with me.

Children feel this type of pride about their family. Together, they share experiences that no one else can replicate or fully understand. What happens inside the walls of their home is sacred, and it solidifies a kind of group posture—one of togetherness and teamwork.

Have you ever wondered why a group of lions is called a pride? Lions are labeled this way not because they are arrogant, insecure, and boastful animals, but because they fight fiercely to protect their own. According to the National Geographic Society, "Lions are the only big cats to live in family units called prides. . . . A lion pride may include up to three males, a dozen females, and their young. All of the pride's female lionesses and cubs are typically related. . . . The social structure of the pride is based on specific roles. Lionesses are the primary hunters, while dominant males are responsible for protecting the pride's territory."[1]

This is the kind of pride children want to feel in their families—the type of pride that is strong, steadfast, and will spur the family to do anything to protect its members. They stay together no matter the threat. When they are with their family members, they feel secure. The family pride is a protective factor that communicates to all its members that nothing will disrupt their team. My family functioned this way for many years. We took pride in identifying as a unit, and my parents regularly reinforced this value in our upbringing. Our family members felt healthy, valued, and committed.

Sometimes communication patterns are easily distinguished as dangerous, and children can see divorce coming. In my experience, however, the initial separation announcement came as a complete surprise. We children were brokenhearted and confused. For many years I felt stuck in denial, believing that this was not our family's forever story and that eventually the cloud of confusion would disappear. I held on to hope that our family would reunite and be stronger than before.

Divorce threatens a family's pride, and to mediate the fall, parents share their reasons and justifications with their new spouses. If you're married to someone who has been divorced, do you remember the reasons you were told to justify the *why* behind their divorce? What messages did these explanations etch on your spirit? Did you hear about how selfish or angry or high-maintenance the former spouse was? Did you listen with empathy, and maybe even feel sorry for your spouse? Did any part of you feel motivated to right all the wrongs and promise to never make your spouse live with such hurt?

The narratives you hear can sometimes further the tension between you and your stepchildren. Children don't know or believe the same narrative you accept as reality. That selfish person who made life so painful for your now-spouse is their mom or dad. From their perspective, there is no evil in either one. Justifications for divorce are commonly shared with you as a spouse, and each story line you hear becomes data in forming a narrative about why divorce was necessary. These narratives shape a new spouse's beliefs about the former spouse, and they sometimes inadvertently create distance between stepparent and stepchild. A stepparent takes immense pride in his or her role in a new marriage and may feel their own familial pride stirring to want to protect the children from an ex who put their spouse through so much pain. Even if nothing is ever verbalized, children are very aware and can feel the disdain you may have for their biological mom or dad. As a result, they may distance themselves from you.

Think back on the reasons you were given for the divorce. Explanations might range from mental illness to infidelity; each situation is unique for every couple experiencing the painful process. It is not your role as a stepparent to share with the children what you heard about the *why*. Still, many children inquire about why this is happening to them. Looking to my own experience, and drawing from stories other children have shared with me, there are three common justifications parents might share with their new spouse to explain why they got divorced. Think about whether any of these reasons were part of the narrative you were told and how this impacts family dynamics. I'll share a few ideas about why stepchildren fight each justification and, in turn, sometimes fight with you.

"We never really loved each other"

I remember talking with a high school student I knew through a youth outreach organization. She shared with me a conversation that occurred shortly after her parents finalized their divorce. I empathized with her, as she was the same age I had been when I experienced this story line in my life. She was halfway through her junior year and in the crux of the college selection process, so I invited her to grab a milkshake and get an update on her frontrunners. She had recently returned from a scouting trip she took with her dad to tour some of the East Coast schools on her list.

"Can you believe junior year is almost over?" I asked. "It is so crazy to think you only have one more year before you make your mark in the big leagues. I feel like you just got your braces off and were asking me about class schedules, and now you're submitting your college applications. How are you handling all of this, especially considering your parents' divorce? Did you have fun on your trip? Which school was your favorite?" The conversation quickly shifted from schools to her family, and she shared some of the conversations she had with her dad.

"The schools were fine. Time with my dad was fine. It was good but also really hard."

"What was hard about it?" I asked.

"I just heard some things that I wish I didn't hear."

"Like what?" She answered by repeating some of the conversations her dad shared to help her understand why her parents divorced. The details of one conversation really stuck with me.

"He told me that he never really loved my mom but always thought she was beautiful." Her father's words were not intended to cause pain, but they did. She went on to explain to me her fear of some guy pursuing her because of her looks and then choosing to leave her if she was not able to maintain the things that initially attracted him. If her mom had stayed active and maintained an athletic build, would they still be together? If she had tightened her wrinkling skin with Botox and worn the latest fashion trends, would he still be attracted to her? Her father's justification did not offer peace but rather rooted in her a spirit of fear, for she was processing a superficial relationship based on selfish infatuation and not on selfless love.

Was the "we never really loved each other" narrative part of the story you heard before marrying your stepchild's mom or dad? If so, you may subconsciously feel the responsibility to make up for all the "loveless" years and appear to overcompensate in the eyes of the child. From a child's perspective, his or her parents did love one another, and many of them saw plenty of evidence of kindness and affection displayed to affirm it. It is common for stepparents to feel sad that kids had to grow up in a difficult and conflict-ridden household; however, for many, the toxicity didn't even begin until the divorce occurred. Therefore, in a child's eyes, the stepparent role is not viewed as a solution to a problem but rather as a problem itself.

The reasoning and decision-making mechanism in the brain, the prefrontal cortex, is not fully developed until age twenty-five. Therefore, it is unrealistic to expect that children will be able to differentiate the healthy dynamics of a parent's remarriage from the unhealthy parts of their former nuclear family. Children do not process divorce from a logical perspective. Instead, they respond to what they feel. They don't immediately feel grateful that their parent or parents found someone new who loves them well. Instead, they feel confused and hurt, because what they knew as a loving family ended. While your spouse sees you as a redemptive love in his or her life, a child sees the same story as the deterioration of a former love. Because these perspectives are in conflict, your selfless and sincere mission to restore a child's broken love story is sometimes received as part of the brokenness.

Children do eventually become adults, and their brains fully develop with more mature reasoning skills. As this happens, they can look at the data and assess for themselves whether your marriage really is healthier than the previous marriage of their biological parents. Unfortunately, this likely will not occur in your current parenting season. Refrain from the temptation to prove your love by working harder or trying to convince the children that this marriage is better. Accepting this as truth, in a child's eyes, destroys the familial pride that he or she innately fights to maintain. The ultimate desire of a stepparent is that a shift may happen, and the kids may begin to fight for you and not against you. With time—and steadfastness on your part—children may come around and affirm you well. My heart took a long time to get to this point, but my current mindset toward my stepparents is one of appreciation. I want each of them to know I am grateful that they love my parents well.

"We tried everything; it just didn't work"

Have you ever met someone with "looking disease"? Before you answer this question, let me describe some of the disease's symptoms. Before I had children, I had never met anyone with this condition. But after becoming a parent, I realized both of my kids had this diagnosis. How did I know? One morning, after my daughter complained about not being able to locate her left shoe, I sent her with simple instructions for finding it.

"I'm sorry to hear it is lost. Go retrace your steps, and look around where you last remember taking it off."

"Okay, Mom," she responded. About five minutes went by, and then, inevitably, her voice echoed over the banister. "I still can't find it!" I remembered a tactic my parents tried when we were young, and said, "Okay, well, if I come up and find it, there will be a consequence." Her feet quickly pitter-pattered back to the path of discovery. The shoe was exposed on her bedroom floor in plain sight, in the very spot she had looked just minutes earlier. I've come to discover that every member of my family has symptoms of this disease. You lose something, and when you try to find it, the object is overlooked. Usually, looking disease upsets me. I get frustrated when people do not make a concerted effort to seek until the lost item is found. I used to get angry and frustrated. These days, instead of getting angry, I repeat a famous line from Disney's *The Lion King*. When Simba fails to see his dad in the reflection pond, Rafiki, his wise baboon mentor, skims the pond with his walking stick and says, "Look harder." After one more concentrated effort, Simba focuses on his reflection and finds his father in the image on the water. He sees, as if for the first time, that his father's legacy still lives within him.

What does looking disease have to do with stepparenting? It helps explain the exhaustion you feel when you are trying everything but still feel that nothing you are doing is working. There is still a huge wall between you and the stepchildren, and you want more than anything for the wall to fall. You feel pride in your role and want the children to embrace this pride with you to begin gaining traction with a new family identity. You see very clearly why your marriage is a healthier setup for the kids and begin to replay the narratives you were told to help kids understand that your blended family really is beneficial. One of these narratives might sound like this: "I know your parents really did try everything, and sadly, it just didn't work." Children fight this narrative and don't easily accept it as a justification. Children of divorce are skeptical when they hear, "They tried everything." It is like my kids saying, "We looked everywhere." It is impossible for them to have looked everywhere, for if they had, they certainly would have found their lost item. Instead of saying, "Your parents really did try everything," consider framing your narrative with a surprising opportunity for compassion: "I know your parents wanted to make it work. I heard that they both committed to counseling. That must have been a difficult and challenging season for you to process. I'm sad your parents did end up divorcing. I really believe they gave it their best effort."

If children hear that even their stepparents would have preferred for them to avoid the pain of divorce, it builds empathy, and kids begin to trust that you understand that the situation they are in is not ideal. Some of the stories children tell themselves about their stepparents sound something like this:

You did this to our family. You wanted my parents to split up. If it weren't for you, my parents would still be together. If you were not involved with the biological parent pre-divorce, these thoughts are not fair and are not rooted in truth. However, these perceptions are real for kids, and they make connecting with you nearly impossible. Even if you met your spouse long after the divorce was final, most stepparents would choose to spare their stepchildren from the pain they experienced because of it. Sharing this hope with stepchildren is a surprising way to demonstrate your sincere desire to protect them and not to harm them. It shows the children that you know divorce is not the ideal design for a family, yet you are committed to making the best of the circumstance and reclaiming hope in place of regret.

In some cases, relationships do begin before a divorce is finalized. In these circumstances, children's perceptions are not speculative but are very real. Infidelity wreaks havoc on a family, and part of the pain that ensues can manifest in how children respond to the parent(s) involved. God has the power to redeem even the most painful circumstances. Redemption, however, does not come without the pain of the cross. The hurts children and parents feel in the case of infidelity cannot be overlooked. God, however, knows extreme pain and is faithful to heal if we take ownership of our sin. "If we confess our sins, he is faithful and just and will forgive us our sins and purify us from all unrighteousness" (1 John 1:9).

Modeling this verse is one of the most difficult and humbling experiences for a follower of Christ, yet the results of obedience are some of the most powerful.

"God had a different plan for our family"

Since childhood, I have loved writing, and I still remember stories I crafted in elementary school and illustrated with watercolor paint and Crayola markers. This passion continued through middle school. My friend Ashley and I bought a journal at the mall, and like long-distance pen pals, we wrote daily journal entries, trading off at the end of each school week. This journaling habit played a key role in my early years of faith. In my adolescent years, praises became passionate petitions on the pages as I begged God to change the outcome of my parents' divorce.

Seeing God as good was a struggle in the aftermath. I perused my Bible's concordance to find a way to understand it all, and all I could find was, "For I hate divorce" (see Malachi 2:16 NLT). A fierce spiritual war was waged in my heart as I read these words; my parents, who said they loved God, were going through with something God clearly said He hates. I've come to recognize that one of the reasons God hates divorce is because of the tremendous pain it causes in relationships. God sees the parents' pain, and He sees the children's pain. His compassion doesn't stop there. He knows and sees the stepparents' pain as well.

He grieves that the consequences of someone else's divorce directly affect you. God hates divorce; He does not hate the divorced. He sees you. He sees each insult and eye-roll from your stepchildren, and it breaks His heart. He sees regret and shame that make parents feel like they've failed, and He weeps. He sees children struggle to understand their new family dynamic, and He grieves.

In attempts to embrace the redemptive power of forgiveness and second chances, sometimes believers place responsibility for pain on God himself. They say things like, "Our blended family is part of God's perfect plan." Avoid using this kind of language to get closer to your stepchildren. It may backfire and create even further distance. Children who grew up in the church and experienced divorce already wrestle with the reality that their faith in God was not enough to save their parents' marriage, so when they hear from their stepparents that God planned this as their family's story, there is internal tension: *If God hates divorce, why would He not only let it happen, but plan it this way? If He is good, why is our family broken?*

Rather than defining your blended family as God's perfect plan, take advantage of an opportunity to speak about His sovereign character—character that remains the same regardless of our difficult circumstances. Share with the kids that God never designed your family to feel fragmented. He hates that they've endured all the grief and change that came with a decision they didn't make. He is also sad and wants their heart to heal. The pain they have experienced is not because of God, but because people are imperfect. God's grace, however, allows all of us to come through the pain with higher perspective and second chances. Your blended family provides an opportunity for experiencing second chances and redeeming love. As a stepparent, verbalize your commitment to seeking God's help to find healing in something that has caused your stepchildren a lot of pain. This transparent posture that owns the brokenness of the situation is much more successful than trying to justify the situation as God's idea in the first place.

Remember that it is tempting to rely on the narrative you hear from your spouse to explain and justify the *why* behind his or her divorce. Children, however, often hold on to a very different narrative, one that is rooted in a familial pride that fights to protect what used to be, rather than accepting what is.

Keep the door open for hearing both sides of the narrative, and surprise your stepchildren with elements of their stories that you also grieve and wish you had the power to change.

------------------------------ CHAPTER 8 ------------------------------
TAKEAWAY SUMMARY

1. Remember the power that pride plays for children clinging to a past family identity. They are typically not ashamed of their family's heritage and fight to hold on to the good. This internal fight creates additional barriers that sometimes lengthen the time necessary to bond with a new family legacy.

2. Consider the justification narrative you may believe after conversations your spouse has shared regarding his or her former partner. Be careful not to assume that the children share the same perspective.

9

Memory Loss

When something is hidden, trashed, or destroyed, it is indicative of something bad or shameful. These labels often flood a child's mind as he or she processes what is permissible in memorializing the pre-divorce family picture.

My family highly prioritizes adventure. When it comes to wish lists for gift-giving occasions, you'll find ours peppered with gear and equipment for outdoor activities. We draft bucket lists of travel destinations or tickets for unique events. For me, nothing says romance like the gift of gear. Josh knows to skip the jewelry store or florist and head straight to the latest outdoor-enthusiast retail location. Our wedding registry was devoid of china place settings; instead, we opted for his-and-her headlamps, camping sleeping pads, and a tent for two. We've expanded beyond the camping basics with wet suits and scuba masks, climbing harnesses and snowshoes. Why? Because in our hierarchy of values, memories trump materials.

Memories are the building blocks of a family legacy. Adventures occur and are retold around fire pits, kitchen islands, and bunk beds. These memories mark a family with unified experiences, bonding each with a "remember when" highlight reel. We want the answers to our remember-when conversations to finish with details involving love and laughter. I've yet to find value in a remember-when story that ended with "you bought me that flashy diamond bracelet." Instead, I delight in those that sound more like, "Remember when we were all on a fishing boat about to fall asleep and head back to shore, when suddenly, we sprang to our feet after watching one of the rods disappear deep under the boat? After more than an hour of teamwork and eager anticipation, we experienced the thrill of catching an eight-foot shark."

These are the memories life is made of, and the stories they create will live on as family connectors for generations to come. The account of the shark catch happened on a trip with my mom and stepdad and will forever be something I cherish. My siblings and stepdad all have something very special to share because of the commitment our family has made to invest in experiences over things. These memories are the fruit of a determination to forge and follow newfound traditions as a blended family. Moments like this were not always celebrated in the early years of our blended family experience. Before newfound memories and traditions could be created, it was necessary to allow healing from the grief that accompanied the memory loss suffered after divorce.

If you have ever witnessed a loved one's memory loss, you understand the difficulty and sadness that ensue. Many people have shared stories with me about a family member suffering from Alzheimer's disease, but until recently, I had never experienced the emotional struggle firsthand. A few years ago, I received a call about my grandfather and learned that he had recently survived a stroke. His brain injury was severe and stole much of Grandpa's physical health. The most difficult loss, however, was that of his memory. I had the opportunity to visit him during the weeks following the injury. My heart leapt with joy to see his smile as his warm eyes met mine in his hospital room.

"Hi, Grandpa!" My greeting was reciprocated, but not the way I might have imagined. He didn't recognize me without a formal introduction and reminder.

"Hey, Grandpa, it's Lauren," I announced. My siblings shared their names as well. Although we stood before him, Grandpa needed his memory jogged to restore what was once easy to identify as normal and familiar. Those next three days were sacred. My brothers and sister gathered with me around his hospital bed and shared our remember-whens with Grandpa. He had no memory of the present or short-term happenings, yet he could recall with incredible accuracy the details of his life long ago.

"I shouldn't be in this bed," Grandpa muttered during one such conversation. "I should be on a horse!"

"You're right, Grandpa. You were the best cowboy I ever knew!" I kissed his forehead that night and embraced him with a hug that would be my last. He may not have known my presence in that moment, but reminiscing in the glory of the good old days helped affirm hope that Grandpa did remember. I treasure the opportunity to sit in his presence and recall the moments that marked my life with his love.

Something about Grandpa's recollection of riding a horse on the ranch made the pain of his memory loss more bearable. His storytelling gave me a glimpse into his mind and his heart, and it reassured me that he had the capacity to recollect the best parts of his earlier years. There is an art to storytelling that keeps memories alive and enables those of us following a previous legacy to know the depth and experience that meant so much to our predecessors. Although Grandpa was not aware of the gift he gave me by speaking about the horses, his recollection served as a redemptive piece of my heritage. This reminded me of one of the unexpected struggles children may encounter after one or both of their parents remarry—memory loss.

Removing Reminiscence

Sometimes I miss the anticipation that used to follow a photo-worthy event. I remember standing in line at our local grocery-store film counter, holding the claim ticket I filled out days prior as I left my sealed envelope containing a roll of 35mm film. When they had called to let me know my pictures were ready, I leapt to my feet and begged my mom to drive me straight to the pick-up counter.

"I have to see them!" I exclaimed. "Please, can we go now?" I hovered over my mom and even inquired about tasks I could help her finish to speed our departure. Very soon I'd have a fresh stack of prints to flip through. To me, picture pick-up days were about more than seeing images of events past; they marked the opportunity to gather with important people I loved and reminisce over each detail.

My sixteenth birthday was celebrated with gusto. Trays of homemade lasagna lined a buffet table at the Crystal Rose Conference Center where my friends gathered for the festivities. The tables were lined with butcher paper and crayons. Guests sketched outlines of the number sixteen and wrote complimentary re-marks that I enjoyed reading as I floated around the room. There were beach balls to volley and beanbags to toss. Crowds gathered on the dance floor, and before cake was served, everyone sat with attention toward a screen playing a slideshow of photos from my childhood. I still remember sitting in the crowd, flashing my braces-clad smile in Gap denim overalls. That smile was forever captured after the flash of one of the many disposable cameras that were peppered throughout the party. Those cardboard-box film containers were the most valuable takeaway from the event. The printed photographs landed on the pages of a photo album, which now sits on a shelf at one of my parents' homes.

Before the divorce, we used to take photo albums off the shelf and flip through the pages on the couch with Mom and Dad, pointing to the images that invited further detail and discussion. The younger years sparked most of our curiosity, as we weren't old enough to recollect the details. It was enjoyable to hear our parents share the background information, illuminating the experience as if it were happening all over again. Reminiscing served as a reminder for all of us to gain knowledge about our family history. Without these stories, we would lose the ability to fully develop our memory and have the capacity to share these special moments with our own families in the future.

After blending our families, our nuclear family pictures and albums were moved from coffee tables and family room book-shelves and stored in basement corners. This reorganization was necessary and even helpful for all of us to move forward in accepting the changes that marked our new family structure. This practice, however, removed reminiscence as a permissible family routine. Children understand the practicality of this decision. There are new people in your family who need and deserve a space in your future photo albums, but the pages for children often are forced to begin anew, blank without permission to publicly remember their past. Granted, there were not locks on the photo albums, nor did anyone in either family condemn or communicate restrictive rules around viewing old family photos, but the pastime subconsciously transitioned from a public to a private affair. It felt taboo and hurtful to march with old family pictures to the living room couch and invite the new stepparent and biological parent to gather around for story time. Neither adult craved a memory jog of that past life. For them, creating a new family picture required freedom for a fresh start—one that contained blank pages for writing a new chapter, not previously populated pictures.

A similar picture purge happens with family photos around the house. Currently, in our home, a silver frame holds a large picture of our Reitsema family. Capturing this image was no small feat. We braved the crisp Colorado cold and positioned our three- and one-year-old children on laps atop a boulder in the middle of a white-water river running through a canyon in the Rocky Mountains. Our pockets were stuffed with Skittles in case we needed a little sugar rush to aid in the smile department. Surprisingly, we ended up with four beaming smiles and eye contact from all without even tapping in to our candy stash. The miracle of that moment forever remains above our fireplace mantel, and when guests come over or our kids are curious, we take delight in telling the details of that adventure.

In my present state of mind, the first thought I have when gazing at our river photo is, *Why did we invest in a family picture of that size when we knew we wanted another baby?* Being pregnant, I am acutely aware that soon we will need to replace that family picture with one picturing a family of five. My heart is wired for justice and fairness, and I cannot imagine explaining to our future child that Daddy and I didn't want to spend the time or money to update our family mantel picture, so baby number three will just have to deal with the image of the family as it existed prior to his or her arrival.

This was a far cry from my heart's desire. There is so much excitement and anticipation surrounding the growth of our family, and nothing will stop us from replacing the old with the new and improved version coming this fall. Josh and I do plan to update our family photo, but the current version will still exist and simply be repositioned elsewhere so we can enjoy it as the before-baby version of our growing family. In a blended family context, however, these sentiments are processed and felt a bit differently.

Missing the Mantelpiece

In a biological nuclear family, adding a family member repositions the older version of the image hanging above the mantel. In a blended family, however, there is not a reposition but rather a replacement. It would be insensitive to hang nuclear family photos in the home after remarrying a new spouse. Children of divorce don't want to hang this picture anywhere either. It feels strange to memorialize a photo of their former family. Doing so only fosters continued triggers for hurt. What happens to the before-divorce version of a family photo? Is it hidden? Is it thrown away? Is it destroyed? Each choice for what to do with this physical memory reflects what can happen to the emotional picture for a child of divorce. Rather than simply shifting the picture's position because of a new family dynamic, children in blended families feel they must hide, trash, or destroy the old. When something is hidden, trashed, or destroyed, it is indicative of something bad or shameful. These labels often flood a child's mind as he or she processes what is permissible in memorializing their pre-divorce family picture. Thoughts such as, *Am I allowed to feel good about my old family picture? Can I talk about this family in front of my stepparents? Are these memories allowed but supposed to be kept private?* or *Are these memories something I just throw away and forget from this point forward?* flood their minds.

Without open dialogue and clear expectations, the answers to these questions remain a mystery. Sometimes children immediately assume the rules that apply to the mantel picture also apply to them. Hide it, trash it, or destroy it. As the photo goes missing, family memories leave with it. With limited freedom to reminisce and images from the past hidden, children forget pieces of their childhood. There is grace when the memory loss involves painful memories, but there is sadness when the good times are also forgotten. As a stepparent, you can help provide answers for children to process this transition without attaching it to shame. There are two strategies I recommend for helping your stepchildren better cope with memory loss and for creating positive new memories while moving forward in your blended family's journey. The first is to openly embrace taboo topics, and the second is to establish and treasure traditions.

Talk through Taboo

It is natural to pursue a problem-solution methodology when preparing for and coping with life's unexpected challenges. For financial woes, there are strategic classes designed to equip families to eliminate debt. When students struggle in school, parents can research tutoring options or seek help from a teacher to outline a plan for improvement. When you don't make a sports team, programs exist to build strength and outline dietary disciplines for better performance at the next tryouts. When confronted with someone else's pain, however, there is no how-to manual.

A knock on my front door usually means one of two things: a neighbor's child is soliciting a cul-de-sac playdate, or a lawn care specialist is testing a sales pitch for aeration services. I try to say yes to the first and no to the latter. There recently was an instance in which neither answer applied to the circumstance: I opened my door to discover a neighbor with a facial expression I hadn't seen before. Grieving and downtrodden, she shared the news that our mutual friend had just tragically lost her teenage daughter.

"She's gone," she explained. "What do we do?" I'll never forget the shock and sadness that followed this announcement. Nothing we could say or do would change the fact that someone we care about was experiencing unprecedented heartache. We could cook, offer to help with household tasks, send flowers, attend the service, or express our sympathy in a card. Nothing, however, would change her pain. During the days that followed, I felt paralyzed with fear every time I saw her family. *What do I say? How do I respond? Do I make eye contact?* In this situation, I felt there was no right answer. After about a week of my awkward avoidance strategies, I felt convicted to confront my fear.

The next family member I saw was the teen's grandmother. This time, instead of my usual evasion, I opted for telling the truth. "Hi, Katie," I greeted her. "I want to be honest and let you know that my heart deeply aches for your family after hearing about your loss. I wish I had something to say that could help the situation. I want to be able to offer something that will make it better. I'm embarrassed to admit it, but I've been avoiding a conversation because I feel nervous to approach you without being able to offer help. Can you help me learn the best way to support you? Are you free to come over for coffee and simply talk?"

"You have no idea how much I would enjoy that," she responded. "Tell me when, and I'm there." We found a time in our schedules that would work. I steeped my favorite New Mexican roast and applied pressure to the metal coffee filter of my French press. I topped two mugs with a frothy vanilla creamer and carried the homemade lattes into the living room. We sat and sipped and shared life. I asked questions I might typically avoid. Topics that felt taboo became turning points in our relationship. When I felt afraid to broach a subject, I vocalized my fear and followed my statements by giving her the freedom to pass on any question that felt inappropriate or unsafe.

Before this conversation, I had made too many assumptions about what was permissible to discuss and what was off-limits. My assumptions had created a wedge between us rather than serving as the bridge I believed my boundaries would build. I began to feel more secure, and what I felt was a hopeless situation suddenly inspired hope. Yes, the conversation was uncomfortable, but embracing the discomfort brought Katie the very comfort she needed.

Have you ever found yourself in this position with your stepchildren? Have you desired to understand their pain or perspective but felt the topic was taboo? If so, you are not alone. In my experience, it felt dishonoring or even rude to explore the difficult transitions in blending my family with the people who now held the role of stepparent. I felt that if I were to express my pain or the difficulty in the transition, it would increase their hurt or cause tension and division. I had the mindset that avoiding my process was the only safe and polite way to handle it. The problem with this philosophy, however, was that it led to a relationship built upon assumptions rather than honest conversation.

I made assumptions about what my stepparents were thinking; I assumed they made assumptions about what I was thinking. And after collecting our data from an assumptive posture, we lost the ability to speak truthfully. My biological parents found themselves in the middle of triangulated conversations. I would run to my parents with complaints about their new spouses, and my stepparents would unload their angst and hurt regarding my selfish and difficult behavior. What usually ensued was a private lecture between bio-parent and child, instructing me to be more kind and explaining their distaste for my selfish behavior. I was not present for the conversation between spouses, but I imagine the dialogue taking on similar themes, with stepparents asked to be patient with the process and explanations that this struggle hadn't been easy on anyone involved.

A similar story came to my attention after speaking at a blended family event. After closing out the workshop, I packed up my materials to head to the airport. Before I made it to my car, a gentleman stopped me to ask my advice about a situation he was navigating with his daughter.

He shared the celebratory news that his daughter was approaching her due date with his very first grandchild, but the joyous occasion felt shadowed by the high-pressure stakes surrounding the blended family expectations for the hospital visit. He shared his concern about his wife (his daughter's stepmother) wanting to honor boundaries and not create unnecessary conflict or division with his former wife and her new spouse in the waiting room. He unpacked the details and shared snippets of dialogue and negotiation about the grandparent conversations. Visibly distraught, he sought my perspective.

"In your opinion, what do you think is the best way to support our daughter?" I was humbled by his faith in me, and understood the intention he put behind his ask. It was clear that his ultimate goal was to minimize the difficulty that blended family dynamics can bring to these milestone moments and to support his daughter as a first priority. I recognize the frustration that follows when a question is answered with a question, but in this situation, it was necessary.

"Have you asked your daughter what she wants?" As he pondered my reply, he realized that to avoid burdening his daughter with post-divorce stress, he and his former wife were navigating all the details and making decisions without directly asking her what she wanted. In an effort to protect her from being in the middle, he was carrying the weight of formulating a plan based on assumptions about his daughter's wishes.

"This experience is one of life's best for your daughter," I added. "If I were to advise you from my perspective, I'd call her and discuss what she wants from both of you." The risk in going to the source to gather expectations is that both parties must be willing to honor the outlined wishes, even if they do not line up with your intended plan. His daughter's response may engender hurt feelings. She might not want either party there, or she may want both there at the same time. She may prefer that only her biological parents visit during the hospital stay, or she may invite stepparents into the mix. It might be better for her to see only one side of the family in the beginning and introduce the baby to the other side in a different setting. I had no way of knowing which direction his daughter's wishes would go, but my hope was to see this adoring father postured to talk through the taboo. Addressing his daughter's wants directly is a helpful alternative to negotiating the details without her voice.

Biological parents, stepparents, and stepchildren all have questions about what the other is thinking or feeling. The insecurities and sensitivities involved in verifying the truth about where each person is coming from subconsciously affirm conversation topics as taboo. Avoiding difficult conversations is a more natural response than confronting them. As this pattern repeats itself, blended family members develop assumptions to help justify or make sense of their decision-making process. Thoughts such as, *They probably don't want me around anyway,* or *No one even notices the effort I'm making in this relationship,* take root as objective data that direct attitudes, actions, and behaviors. Assumptions are not objective truths but rather are subjective opinions. When family members skirt around taboo topics, they are left with only their own thoughts to determine what they see as absolute truth. Often these guessing games are not an accurate depiction of what each person is thinking or feeling. The only way to break through assumptive realities is to clarify with the source. Rather than assuming what is best for your stepchildren, let them give voice to their desires with direct conversation. Tackling taboo subjects is not without risk, yet speaking the truth is often worth it.

Treasure Traditions

Many of the routines and traditions children are accustomed to before your family blends will disappear or dwindle after blending. As discussed previously in this chapter, this stems from the sensitivities and shame children feel when bringing their past experiences into their present realities. Children recognize that everything is different than it was before, and even though they long to cling to what's familiar, the tension they experience causes more stress than the pain of letting go. I remember finding a stained-glass piece at an artisan market that I ended up purchasing for my mom. It was an image of a young girl taking strides on a path leading to a gorgeous mountain meadow. She carried a wooden stick over her shoulder to which was tied a red bandana containing her belongings for the journey. The artist featured only the back of the young woman; her face was not shown. Across the base of the piece read the words *Don't Look Back.* Presenting this gift served as a physical surrender of my own fight. Something in me needed to embrace this sentiment to lessen the burden I carried while clinging to a past that was no longer. This artwork remains in her home today and serves as a hopeful reminder that the lost memories, although they cannot be replaced, can be redeemed.

Evidence of redemptive memories surface every year for my blended family on Christmas Eve. Our first Christmas with my stepdad introduced a tradition he loved: shrimp and tenderloin fondue. Aromatic scents filled the kitchen as he stirred his signature dipping sauces and prepped the fondue pots with oil. We gathered around the table, and my mom prayed a blessing, thanking God for new beginnings as a family. My heart was not yet feeling sincerity about the gratitude part, yet I did enjoy a delicious meal. My stepdad shared something that was originally his; now it had become ours. Christmas Eve fondue has become one of the highlights of each year. I am no longer reluctant to join but rather eager to attend. Maintaining this tradition helped us maintain our identity as a blended family.

One year, my stepdad thought it would be fun for my grandmother to take the lead for the Christmas Eve dinner and asked her to prepare a traditional Italian feast. From his perspective, inviting her heritage and spotlighting her as the chef felt like a way to honor our family's roots. Word of the adjustment quickly began to spread among my siblings. My phone lit up with text messages, each echoing frustrated, and even angry, sentiments. *Lasagna on Christmas Eve? What is he thinking? Did one of you tell him to change it?* The complaints eventually made it to my mom, and she was surprised by all the pushback.

"Why is everyone so upset?" she asked. "It's just food."

"Mom," I explained. "Christmas Eve is the one tradition that has been constant since you two got married. We can count on it happening every year. It's something we have all grown to love. This has nothing to do with food." The backlash from this incident clearly communicated the power of honoring treasured traditions as a blended family. I honestly can't remember what we used to eat for Christmas before the divorce. Recollecting the past is difficult, but now I wait with eager anticipation each year as Christmas Eve approaches. Lingering around steaming fondue pots and reminiscing together is something special. This treasured tradition helped play a role in redeeming my lost memories and restoring them with present memories I can forever cherish.

Consider the family traditions in your blended family. Are there any recurring events you can count on each year? If so, be aware of their value and do your best to commit to keeping them. If you have yet to establish traditions, invite a dialogue with your family to set a few routines in place. Determining a starting point can feel challenging. There may be initial pushback, but pressing through and prioritizing consistency helps gel a newfound identity. As children juggle multiple family dynamics, maintaining a few routine traditions helps them find continuity and better manage expectations.

--- CHAPTER 9 ---
TAKEAWAY SUMMARY

1. Recognize that embracing a new family picture often steals a child's freedom to reminisce about the old days. Help create safe boundaries to remove shame from their desire to remember.

2. Create an atmosphere of emotional safety to openly address taboo topics.

3. Work to establish and keep traditions that create continuity and security for what children can expect as a family.

10

Future Legacy

> Our family tree appeared to be rooted in strong soil. . . . Yet the patterns
> in my drawing indicated that somewhere the branches split and cracked.
> I worried my future was destined to be the same.

One of the best perks about living in Colorado is experiencing four distinct seasons every year. Winters drop glistening, powdery flakes, providing the perfect setting for downhill ski adventures and epic childhood sledding runs. The snowcapped mountains kiss the sun to welcome spring, bringing life to fields of wildflowers coloring miles of meadows. Summers bring brilliant blue skies and enough sustained sunshine to create the perfect atmosphere for swimming or hiking through the Rockies. Fall makes its entrance right on time as the heat of the summer sun becomes draining. The golden glow of aspen leaves illuminates the skies under crisp, cool air. This always refreshes my soul.

As a mom, one of the most refreshing things about the onset of fall is welcoming back-to-school season. That first day approaches just after crossing the last activities off the summer bucket list and just before most parents run out of mediation skills for mitigating sibling spats. School supplies cascade out of new backpacks hung in orderly fashion on newly organized cubby hooks. When the first day of school arrives, kids spring from bed, model their preselected outfit, and enjoy a balanced breakfast. Parents place a sign featuring grade levels in each child's hand and snap a quick photo. Hustling to encourage a timely arrival, Mom or Dad steals one last hug and high five, and off the kids go to embrace another year of learning.

My school memories were typically positive ones. I remember having a performance-driven attitude paired with a deep desire to please people. This combination made me a student of my teachers as well as a student of the content of their classes. Language arts and history trumped math and science on my favorites list. The absolutes in math sometimes intimidated me. Formulas may allow flexibility when calculating a final answer, yet a correct result on the right-hand side of the equals sign is nonnegotiable. It was always refreshing to have help from my parents when I struggled to correctly complete my math homework. Now, in my homework-help season for my own children, I am thankful for the simplicity of concepts coming home in their folders. I have confidence in my ability to drill them on multiplication facts and long division. As they progress through the ranks toward calculus, however, I will pass the baton to my brilliant, engineer-minded husband. As for today, I rest assured in my abilities to answer questions from elementary-level packet prep.

I remember some of the first math concepts that turned up in my children's backpacks during their early preschool years. One of the foundational concepts they explored had to do with patterns. As I emptied their backpacks after school, I sorted stacks of crumpled papers showcasing what they practiced during math. Small squares marked with various pictures or shapes had been cut, colored, and glued in a straight line to indicate a pattern.

"Look, Mom!" my preschooler explained. "I glued them in a pattern."

"Great work, honey," I affirmed. "What is the pattern on this page?" I inquired.

"See, it goes apple, worm, bird, apple, worm, bird."

"You're right, sweetheart. Mom is very proud of your work." After affirming a job well done, my daughter or son would then drag a chair over to the bulletin board, select a colorful pushpin from the junk drawer, and proudly place their work on display.

Recognize Patterns

Patterns are one of my favorite math concepts. According to the *Collins English Dictionary*, "A pattern is the repeated or regular way in which something happens or is done."[1] In other words, a pattern is defined by repetition. The only way to break a pattern is to change something about the repeating order of events. After my parents' divorce, I remember looking intently at the familial patterns of my extended family legacy, and what I noticed forced me to pause and reflect on patterns I had not previously seen as influences in my own family's experience. What I discovered was that divorce was a more prominent pattern than that of lasting marriage. I became a little nervous when I reflected on its prevalence in our family tree.

It was no secret that my parents both had divorce in their lineage, yet I had never charted the pattern visually. To better understand possible reasons for my parents' split, I decided to draw our family tree. Pen in hand, I began outlining each branch. Mom's mom split from her husband when my mom and her siblings were little to protect the safety of her young family. Mom's dad was no longer a part of his family's life, and my grandmother never remarried. Her passionate and protective role as the matriarch of a strong, single-parent narrative produced three vibrant and resilient children. All three of Grandma's children married and had children of their own. Two out of the three experienced the heartbreak of divorce in their own marriage journeys.

Dad's branches were anchored by a lasting marriage between Grandma and Grandpa, who also had three children. All three children were married, but each ended up walking through the heartache of divorce. The youngest divorced multiple times and never had children of her own. Both older siblings were part of strong marriages lasting more than fifteen years, but both their marriages ended during my siblings' and cousins' early high school days. Seeing this pattern on paper felt defeating. Before divorce, my parents and aunts and uncles appeared to be in very fulfilling and happy relationships. We all grew up experiencing carefree adventures layered with affection and love. Our family tree appeared to be rooted in strong soil, producing sturdy branches to weather any storm. Yet the patterns in my drawing indicated that somewhere, the branches split and cracked. I worried my future was destined to repeat this same pattern. Maybe the desire to avoid divorce in my future family was not enough to prevent it from happening. Was I destined to repeat this prevalent pattern? Many children from divorced families ask this question as they approach their own dating and partner selection. As stepparents, there are things you may say or do that can either help or hinder a stepchild viewing marriage in a positive light.

Acknowledge Fear

Today's neighborhoods are divided by fences and security systems, yet sometimes, when we take risks to be known, abundant relational blessings follow. A few weeks ago, I helped my kids get their gear out of the garage and followed them to our driveway to oversee the necessary safety protocol that comes when a pack of children gather and say, "Watch what I can do!" on a solid metal scooter. A few other moms must have had this same safety instinct, as they were also outdoors to observe the tricks. I approached the mom squad and joined the conversation. We had started to discuss a collective carpool strategy when my eye caught the glow of my neighbor's diamond engagement ring. Our family had grown very fond of her family, which had recently moved to our street. Our daughters quickly became playmates and helped to entertain and look out for each of their younger brothers.

"Is this a new development?" I asked with enthusiasm as I broke all personal space boundaries and grabbed her hand to take a closer look. "I don't mean to pry, but did you guys decide to get married?" I'd met her boyfriend multiple times in prior encounters and admired the way he cared for and supported her children. I am the first to gawk and celebrate any hint of an upcoming marriage.

"Actually," she replied as she gently guided my hand back to the appropriate acquaintance space bubble, "I've had the ring for a long time, but I just don't think we're ready for marriage." I apologized profusely for pushing the limits of appropriate neighborly conduct and did my best to backpedal with words that might save face and protect any future friendship possibility that still existed.

"I'm so sorry for putting you on the spot," I explained. "I just love seeing you two together and got so excited when I noticed your ring. It's not my place to rush or judge your decisions. I just think marriage is the best and got excited when thinking about you guys taking that step."

"You're okay," she assured. "It is fun to hear you talk so positively about marriage." I quickly steered the conversation back to carpool details and then retreated back inside to escape the scene where I had so blatantly crossed social boundaries.

A few days later, my phone lit up with a text message from this same neighbor. It read: "Are you by chance going to be home this afternoon? I'd love to swing by and connect about something." I immediately began rehearsing my apology speech. It felt clear that the "I'm sorry" had not been enough to smooth over the way I put her on the spot in front of other neighbors with a question I had no business asking in such a public forum. I typed my response—"Sure thing!"—and I quickly moved into hosting action. I scurried around the house picking up clutter and finishing the last of our dirty dishes that were lingering in the sink. I prepped two glasses of ice water and waited for her arrival. The doorbell rang, and I braced for impact. When I opened the door, my neighbor was not holding a grudge, but rather a giant garment bag protecting the newly purchased white wedding dress draped over her arm.

"Is that a wedding dress?" I shrieked with giddy excitement.

"It is!" she assured. "Your comments the other day were just the nudge we needed to take this step. John and I talked that night after our conversation in the cul-de-sac, and we realized we absolutely want marriage for our future. I don't want to be afraid of it anymore. We love each other and want commitment."

"Come on in! I want to hear everything!" She modeled the gown, and we giggled like high school seniors getting ready for the prom. They had decided to surprise their family and the children with the wedding and had asked me to hide the dress until the main event. This spontaneous drop-in illuminated my spirit. I was thrilled to see the confidence emanating from her. She was ready to surrender the lingering fear associated with blending her family and embrace her marriage dream. For a long time, fear had paralyzed their ability to commit. Fear is often misguided by a false understanding that marriage is the catalyst for relational discord. It is appropriate and sometimes helpful to be honest about the fear that accompanies the decision to marry. Be careful, however, not to point to marriage as the problem.

Correctly Appropriate Blame

Fear is a powerful tactic that I believe the enemy uses to taunt people with the false message that marriage is to blame for the decline in relational satisfaction. Thoughts such as, *Our relationship was thriving until we got married*, take root, and people begin to point to marriage as the issue. This mindset is inaccurate. Think about it this way: If a community of sports fans suffered a losing season with their favorite team, the owners and managers feel the hurt of the frustrated fans and gather to address the core issue and work toward building a better team. News conferences are scheduled, and media outlets start a series of fan interviews to help alleviate the constant pain of losing. An entire city of adoring fans eagerly awaits the results of this massive problem-solving effort. Engaging all media outlets, everyone tunes in for the imminent news conference. The team owner approaches the microphone and begins his report with sentiments of gratitude and appreciation.

"Good morning, sports fans. I wanted to begin by saying thank you for your patience in our discovery process. We recognize our team is not performing well and have rallied every resource we can think of to investigate and address the problem. Many of you have been interviewed to share your perspective, and each player has endured a long series of evaluations to assess how to begin winning again. The time has come to share the results of our tedious reports. I am so proud of our detailed and dedicated staff who helped us arrive at this groundbreaking conclusion. The reason we have suffered years of loss on this team has been determined, and we have conclusive evidence that it is our stadium's fault."

I imagine the reaction of the community would seriously question the validity of these findings. The stadium? Really? Aren't the players responsible for their actions on the field? The talent, skills, teamwork, and mindset they bring to the stadium determine what happens on the field. Blaming a stadium for a team's loss is like blaming marriage for all relational strife. Marriage as an institution is not flawed, nor does it automatically set people up for pain. Instead, it is the participants in marriage, the couples themselves, who are responsible for getting a win. This *marriage is the issue* mindset often inhabits the thoughts of children whose parents have divorced. Without accurate information, many are vulnerable to the belief that if they avoid marriage, they avoid relational pain and hurt. Blaming marriage as the leading cause of divorce may not be an accurate way of thinking, but many children of divorce struggle to reprogram this false messaging. Is it accurate to assume that children of divorce are destined to repeat this pattern for themselves? I certainly had some of those fears after hearing statistical evidence that supported this claim. This is a topic worth exploring.

Dr. Renée Peltz Dennison, PhD, and professor at the University of Maryland, had a similar question motivating her own research efforts to explore whether or not there truly was a divorce destiny predicted among children from divorced house-holds. Dennison is a leading expert in relational health issues. In one of her articles featured in *Psychology Today*, she writes:

> After decades of research, and over a decade of marriage, I continue to work to understand exactly how my family of origin affects my current marriage—but I no longer live in fear of the "sleeper" effects of my parents' divorce. After studying and talking to many couples who have successfully navigated a path from parental divorce to personal marital success, I am confident that the fatalistic picture of couplehood for those exposed to parental divorce is flawed, and that the "transmission" of negative relationship outcomes is by no means inevitable. The bottom line is we play an active part in constructing our own marriages, and therefore have an active part in determining their success.
>
> More and more couples are actively constructing their own paths to relationships, and therefore actively determining their own marital fate. Interestingly, coming of age in a time of higher divorce rates in general may have taught the current generation that marriage isn't something that should be entered into lightly. In USA network survey, 73% of respondents believed that couples should take at least one additional step (such as engagement therapy) before being granted a marriage license.[2]

Dr. Dennison's findings help encourage hope for stepchildren as they process their experience and begin to wonder if marriage really can be healthy and last forever. Overcoming the "sleeper effect," as Dennison calls it, takes determination. Children of divorce should not assume that their future marriage will last simply because they don't want to experience the same hurt. To succeed, they must commit to seeking additional relationship skills and resources before entering their marriage covenant. In Dennison's example, she references engagement therapy as a vital step. Her findings remind us that to overcome the statistical risks, children of divorce must learn tools and skills for setting new relational patterns in motion—patterns that are different from the ones they observed in their parents' marriage. How can children overcome the risks represented in the data? They need people to help them understand the trends and take steps to rise above as an outlier. As a stepparent, you might have the opportunity to be one of these people.

Earlier in this chapter I referenced my bias against math as a subject when compared to language arts and history. As a strategy to get ahead of the collegiate math requirements, I enrolled in an advanced-placement (AP) statistics course my senior year of high school. During the course, I discovered a new way to approach the objective and exact nature of the subject. With statistical analysis, there was room for deviations from the norm. Rather than a nonnegotiable right or wrong, there was freedom to explore outliers. As I studied math concepts from this angle, I felt like I had discovered a powerful loophole. In a subject I had previously known to have only one right answer, there was now room for gray.

Statistically, because of the prevalence of divorce in my family, I still was more susceptible to the potential threat of repeating the pattern; however, this new approach to finding the right answer in a math problem gave me great hope. I was determined to be an outlier, to break the pattern rather than repeat it. To accomplish this goal, I needed to work with more intentionality and become a student of skills that would safeguard my future dream. Your stepchildren most likely will approach marriage with a more guarded, and potentially even fearful, mindset. If you are given the opportunity to discuss their fears, be aware of the following common misconceptions.

Debunk the "Right Person" Myth

The "right person" myth affirms that for marriage to work, you must be lucky enough to find the one right match who completes you. It assumes that after you find this person, your marriage will be on track for success. Be cautious about messages you share in your stepparent role that promote this idea. My heart is not to minimize the importance of personal compatibility in any love story. Choosing a partner with whom you share deeply rooted values and goals is an absolute must for marriage to work. Compatibility alone, however, is not enough to sustain a lifetime love.

A healthy marriage does not happen because of magical chemistry; it requires a selfless, sacrificial, surrendered posture. In addition to this, marriage requires that couples develop a skill set to navigate conflict and communication effectively. Unless individuals change their posture and their communication patterns the second time around, they may not experience success. Even though the person in a relationship changes, there is risk that unhealthy patterns remain. In this type of situation, it becomes much more difficult for children to understand and differentiate a healthy marriage from an unhealthy marriage.

As children explore the "why" in their family's divorce narrative, they are likely to hear that one or both parents were not the right fit for marriage to last. This story line does have merit. Dangerous behaviors, competing personality styles, and toxic conflict patterns create environments that are more hurtful than helpful for children. A new person, however, may not be the only change that is needed to heal and sustain a future legacy that lasts. Stepparents occupy this new-person role in a child's post-divorce family structure.

I believe the transformation toward rebuilding a healthy marriage model is less about person and more about posture.

Consider your role as a verb rather than a noun. Instead of simply *being* a better fit, *become* a better fit. Explore resources to improve your communication skills. Learn the patterns of your personality makeup and that of your partner. Commit to honoring and understanding differences rather than attempting to change one another. This mindset helps affirm for your stepchildren that challenges in marriage happen regardless of who it is you choose.

Becoming the right person—rather than *being* the right person—is a process all couples encounter as they learn to die to themselves and serve their partner. This may sound unbalanced or unfair at first glance: *Die to myself so someone else can be served and get all the benefit?* Remember that when both people are working toward doing the same, the marriage thrives. Each partner puts the other first, sacrificially loving one another as Christ modeled in His ministry. Marriage is more than matching; it is ministering. As your stepchildren look to understand what makes you a better match for either their mom or dad, be sure to credit your posture rather than your personhood. This frees children from the paralyzing fear of spending the rest of their lives trying to find their perfect match—someone who will never frustrate them and who will safeguard their future from repeating the painful cycle of divorce. Help them discover the resources they will need to be an outlier in the statistical narrative. Just because their parents divorced does not mean they will automatically repeat the same path.

Reframing "Broken"

There is something so attractive about the story of an under-dog raising a championship trophy and demonstrating hope that people are capable of defeating even the most terrifying opponents. Stories like these create tear-jerking movie scripts, epic sports documentaries, and inspiring novels. Tasting victory makes any struggle feel worthwhile and brings incredible perspective to a past season of suffering. That big win reprograms the negative naysayer mindset to one marked with optimism and hope. A story, previously labeled broken, is now called beautiful.

I recently said good-bye to a class of high school seniors I had been blessed to mentor before they left for college. This experience gave me firsthand exposure to better understand how difficult these good-byes must be for their parents. Before they took off to drive cross-country and set up their dorm rooms, they asked me for my advice about what major to choose. What classes did they need to prioritize? What path should they take to land a future dream job?

When I was in their shoes, the only motivation I had for a future success story was to break the cycle of divorce (when and if I ever had the opportunity to get married). Looking back on my college departure days, I remember asking people the same questions, hoping their answers would light my path to a guaranteed success story. Truth be told, in that season I wasn't even certain about the school I had committed to. I followed a chunk of change offered via scholarship in hopes that having a tuition cushion would pay off. During orientation, we were assigned to small-group study classes called Freshman Seminars. We were presented with a list of topical interests and asked to prioritize our top three. I filled in the bubbles in everything that seemed to have a relationship theme, and was assigned to a class called Interpersonal Communication Strategies.

From the moment my professor distributed the syllabus, I was hooked. Headings like "Navigating Conflict Styles" and "The Science of Compatibility" graced the page, and my heart exploded. *This is why I am here!* I thought. *These are the things I need to learn to change the divorce narrative.*

Shortly after my first few Freshman Seminar classes, I declared a communications studies major, recognizing that this skill set could apply in almost any career field but would really make a difference in my own relationships. When I walked across the commencement stage a few years later, I held my head high with confidence. I was not just taking home a degree, but a full toolbox of communication strategies that I never knew existed prior to my college season. After graduating, I set out to apply everything I learned about relationships in real time. My vocational path allowed me to regularly put these newfound skills into action. Utilizing the tools in a career was fun, yet the real test was yet to come.

Josh and I reconnected when I visited home to celebrate my mom and stepdad's anniversary. I say reconnected because we had known one another in high school. While I was home with my family, Josh invited me on a rock-climbing adventure that he had planned with my brother and a few friends. I arrived at the climbing gym ahead of Josh and was nearing the top of my route when he entered the building.

"Hey, guys," he greeted. When I saw him, I literally fell off the wall. My brother secured the belay rope to protect me from any injuries. My heart raced in a way I had never previously experienced around Josh—this marked the beginning of our dating relationship. I knew early on that his pursuit felt safe. We craved adventure and found that our mutual love for skiing, summiting mountains, and the Broncos felt more fulfilling when we were together.

As conversations took a turn toward exploring a forever, an incredible surge of guilt flooded my spirit. Josh came from a family heritage marked by little to no divorce. I struggled as I navigated this reality. I believed that by pursuing a future with my broken family legacy, he, too, would be forced to navigate the difficult parts of a blended family and, through no fault of his own, inherit all the delicate dynamics that come with it. These beliefs heightened my insecurities and led me to conclude that my broken family would eventually break his confidence in his decision to marry me. Avoiding the topic felt appropriate for a season, but eventually I knew I needed to face my fears and broach the subject head-on.

Palms sweating, heart beating, and stomach churning, I prepared to discuss my fears with my potential future husband. This conversation could be the deal breaker. All the effort we had poured into our relationship may have been in vain. I finally had the courage to express my nerves about his marrying into all the brokenness. His response forever changed my heart.

"Lauren, I am not choosing a life with you *in spite of* your family history. I am choosing a life with you *because of* your family history. Your experience equipped you with compassion, empathy, grace, resilience, and strength. Watching you face your pain directly and find healing and joy assures me of God's redemptive work. Please know that your family is not broken. Your family is blessed. I love both of your parents and deeply value the relationships we have cultivated with your stepparents. They are part of your past. They will be an incredible part of our future. Divorce has not defined you—divorce has refined you. I love you more because of your story. Your family is whole."

Blended Families, Take Heart!

May these same healing words wash over you and refresh your spirit. You are not broken—you are blessed. You are part of a redemptive story written by a God of second chances. Embrace the pain-points and work through them with honest bravery. Recognize that pieces of your heart may continue to sting a little bit for long periods of time. These setbacks do not define you, but rather, they refine you.

In closing, to my own stepparents and to everyone who occupies the role of stepparent, thank you for loving our parents the way they deserve to be loved. Fight for your marriage; the best is yet to come. Please remember, your stepchildren love you too.

— CHAPTER 10 —
TAKEAWAY SUMMARY

1. Take time to recognize patterns in relationships that you have seen end in divorce. If you find yourself in danger of repeating any of the toxic ones, take steps to change those patterns. Work to stop repeating a negative cycle.

2. Be honest about any fears you might have about the longevity and security of your marriage. Address these fears openly, and find truth to overcome these seeds of doubt.

3. Recognize that the imperfections in people are what make marriage challenging, not marriage as an institution itself.

4. Reprogram your blended family label from broken to blessed.

5. Even when it does not feel like it, know that you are loved.

Notes

Chapter 1: A Family Designation

1. Richard Asa, "Remarrying Your Ex: Proceed with Caution," *Chicago Tribune*, October 23, 2012, http://articles.chicagotribune.com/2012-10-23/features/sc-fam-1023-divorce-reunite-20121023_1_divorce-process-couples-relationship.

2. Asa, "Remarrying Your Ex," *Chicago Tribune*.

3. American Academy of Child and Adolescent Psychiatry, "The Depressed Child," *Facts for Families* No. 4, October 1992, updated May 2008, https://www.sfwar.org/pdf/CSA_Youth/YOU_AACAP_10_92.pdf.

4. "Helping Your Child Through a Divorce," KidsHealth.org, January 2015, accessed August 26, 2018, https://kidshealth.org/en/parents/help-child-divorce.html.

Chapter 5: Identity Crisis

1. Steven Covey, *The 7 Habits of Highly Effective People: Powerful Lessons in Personal Change*, 25th Anniversary Edition (New York: Simon & Schuster, 2013), 247.

2. "What Most Influences the Self-Identity of Americans?" Barna Group, March 19, 2015, accessed December 22, 2017, https://www.barna.com/research/what-most-influences-the-self-identity-of-americans/.

3. Greg Lanier, "No, 'Saul the Persecutor' Did Not Become 'Paul the Apostle,'" The Gospel Coalition, October 31, 2017, accessed December 22, 2017, https://www.thegospelcoalition.org/article/no-saul-the-persecutor-did-not-become-paul-the-apostle/.

Chapter 6: Lingering Effects

1. Compass Rose Academy, "From Selfish to Selfless—How to Change Your Teen's World View," CompassRoseAcademy.org blog, September 10, 2018,

https://compassroseacademy.org/from-selfish-to-selfless-how-to-change
-your-teens-world-view/.

2. Cindy Lamothe, "Your Child Is Not Your Confidant," *Washington Post*, March 23, 2017, https://www.washingtonpost.com/news/parenting
/wp/2017/03/23/your-child-is-not-your-confidant/?noredirect=on&utm_term
=.3cb6c2178638.

3. Gary Smalley, "Making Love Last Forever" (Nashville: Thomas Nelson, 1996), 25.

Chapter 8: The Great Wall of Pride

1. Angela M. Cowan, "Kicked Out of the Pride," *National Geographic*, September 21, 2011, https://www.nationalgeographic.org/media/kicked-out
-pride/.

Chapter 10: Future Legacy

1. "Pattern," *Collins English Dictionary*, https://www.collinsdictionary
.com/us/dictionary/english/pattern.

2. Renée Peltz Dennison, "Are Children of Divorce Doomed to Fail?" *Psychology Today*, August 2, 2014, https://www.psychologytoday.com/us/blog
/heart-the-matter/201408/are-children-divorce-doomed-fail.

Lauren Reitsema is Vice President of Strategy and Communications at The Center for Relationship Education and has been a featured speaker at FamilyLife's Blended Summit and Blended and Blessed conferences. Lauren's interest in relationship education began when her parents divorced after almost twenty years of marriage. Seeking to understand better patterns for her own future legacy, she earned a Bachelor of Science degree in Communication Studies from Texas Christian University. Her vocational speaking experience spans more than fifteen years, teaching a variety of relationship skills to youth, adults, and corporate teams. Lauren recognizes that relationships are one of life's most important assets, and she seeks to energize others to prioritize the people in their lives. She and her husband, Josh, love adventuring with their three children. All Colorado natives, they are avid skiers, outdoor enthusiasts, and Broncos fans.